For Common Things

JEDEDIAH PURDY

For Common Things

Irony, Trust, and Commitment in America Today

ALFRED A. KNOPF   *New York*   1999

THIS IS A BORZOI BOOK
PUBLISHED BY ALFRED A. KNOPF, INC.

www.randomhouse.com

Grateful acknowledgment is made to Henry Holt and Company, LLC, for permission to reprint an excerpt from "Mending Wall" from *The Poetry of Robert Frost,* edited by Edward Connery Lathem. Copyright © 1958 by Robert Frost. Copyright © 1967 by Lesley Ballantine Frost. Copyright 1930, 1939, © 1969 by Henry Holt and Company, LLC.

Library of Congress Cataloging-in-Publication Data
Purdy, Jedediah, [date]
For common things : irony, trust, and commitment in America today / Jedediah Purdy.—1st ed.
p.   cm.
Includes bibliographical references and index.
ISBN 0-375-40708-1 (alk. paper)
1. Social participation—United States.   2. Social action—United States.   3. United States—Social conditions—1980–   4. United States—Politics and government—1993–   I. Title.
HN65.P87 1999
302.14'0973—dc21   99-31055
CIP

Manufactured in the United States of America
Published September 8, 1998
Second Printing, October 1999

For my family
and all my other teachers

What is unpronounced
tends to nonexistence.

—*Czeslaw Milosz*

Contents

Preface

This book is a response to an ironic time. Irony has become our marker of worldliness and maturity. The ironic individual practices a style of speech and behavior that avoids all appearance of naivete—of naive devotion, belief, or hope. He subtly protests the inadequacy of the things he says, the gestures he makes, the acts he performs. By the inflection of his voice, the expression of his face, and the motion of his body, he signals that he is aware of all the ways he may be thought silly or jejune, and that he might even think so himself. His wariness becomes a mistrust of language itself. He disowns his own words.

In answer to all that, this book is a plea for the value of declaring hopes that we know to be fragile. It is an argument that those hopes are no less necessary for their fragility, and that permitting ourselves to neglect them is both reckless and impoverishing. My purpose in writing is to take our inhibition seriously, and to ask what would be required to overcome it, to speak earnestly of uncertain hopes.

To do so requires understanding today's ironic manner. There is something fearful in this irony. It is a fear of betrayal, disappointment, and humiliation, and a suspicion that believing, hoping, or caring too much will open us to these. Irony is a way of refusing to rely on such treacherous things. However, there is also something perceptive about irony, and sometimes we must wonder whether the ironist is right. The ironist expresses a perception that the world has grown old, flat, and sterile, and that we are rightly weary of it. There is nothing to delight, move, inspire, or horrify us. Nothing will ever surprise us. Everything we encounter is a remake, a rerelease, a ripoff, or a rerun. We know it all before we see it, because we have seen it all already.

What has so exhausted the world for us? For one, we are all exquisitely self-aware. Around us, commercials mock the very idea of commercials, situation comedies make *being* a sitcom their running joke, and image consultants detail the techniques of designing and marketing a personality as a product. We can have no intimate moment, no private words of affection, empathy, or rebuke that we have not seen pronounced on a thirty-foot screen before an audience of hundreds. We cannot speak of atonement or apology without knowing how those words have been put to cynical, almost morally pornographic use by politicians. Even in solitary encounters with nature, bicycling on a country road or hiking on a mountain path, we reluctant ironists realize that our pleasure in these places has been anticipated by a thousand L. L. Bean catalogues, Ansel Adams calendars, and advertisements promising a portion of the rugged or bucolic life. So we sense an unreal quality in our words and even in our thoughts. They are superficial, they belong to other people and other purposes; they are not ours, and it may be that nothing is properly ours. It is this awareness, and the wish not to rest the weight of our hopes on someone else's stage set, that the ironic attitude expresses.

Irony is a response to something else as well. In roughly the past twenty-five years, politics has gone dead to the imagination. It has ceased being the site of moral and historical drama. It has come to seem petty, tedious, and parochial.

This change would signify less if politics had mattered less than it has in recent decades. However, for more than two hundred years, politics has been among the great sources of inspiration and purpose, giving shape to many lives. From the radical period of the French Revolution onward there has stood the promise that politics can change the human predicament in elemental ways. Politics, on this promise, could erase all the foolish, cruel, maddening accretions of history and replace them with fair and humane arrangements where for the first time people would live as free as they are born. For both the revolutionaries whose ambitions convulsed the world and the crusading reformers of Britain and America, politics was the fulcrum on which women and men could move the lever of history. They needed only a firm place to stand to take up Archimedes' old boast and move the world.

This extraordinary promise attracted the people with the greatest capacity and need for hope, the ones with the keenest sensitivity to suffering and cruelty and the strongest impulse to work against them. Politics was the means by which those who were most keenly aware of what *should* be could turn that moral truth into historical reality. Politics in effect took over the role of religion for many people in both this century and the last. It gave purpose to individual lives. Its aim of remaking the world carried the promise of redemption, both of whole societies and of the long labors of the individuals who worked to change them. Politics was the way to service, to heroism, and to sainthood.

Because its ambitions ran so far and so deep, politics posed questions that were inescapable for serious people. The questions of what sort of country to live in, what kind of men and women to be, how to work, and sometimes even how to love were all ones that politics promised—or threatened—to resolve. The German author Thomas Mann expressed a widely shared perception, which was sometimes reluctant and sometimes enthusiastic, when he wrote, "In our time, the question of man's destiny presents itself in political terms." Not acknowledging that truth meant avoiding the leading drama of the time.

All of that is now so thoroughly gone that it is difficult even to recall. If it is difficult to speak earnestly of personal matters, to speak earnestly about public issues seems perverse: not only naive, but wrongly or confusedly motivated. Politics is now presumed to be the realm of dishonest speech and bad motives. Moreover, it is accepted that everyone sees through the speech, that the motives are as transparent as the new clothes of the fabled emperor. Public life takes on a quality of unbelievable ritual incredulously performed, like the ceremonies of an aged and failing faith, conducted with the old litanies because no others are available and because rote speech is indifferent to its content anyway.

Our private wariness and the public failure of politics are among the sources of our ironic attitude. Understanding them, describing and diagnosing irony, is one of the things that I attempt to do in this book, and is the concern of the first two chapters. The rest of the book is an attempt to express a hope that seems to me too important to let go unacknowledged. I do not believe that, even where it is strongest, irony has convinced us that nothing is real, true, or ours. We believe, when we let ourselves, that there are things we can trust, people we can care for, words we can say in earnest. Irony makes us wary and abashed in our belief. We do not want the things in which we trust to be debunked, belittled, torn down, and we are not sure that they will be safe in the harsh light of a reflexively skeptical time. Nor can we stand the thought that they might be trivialized, brought into someone's ad campaign, movie dialogue, or self-help phrase. So we keep our best hopes safe in the dark of our own unexpressed sentiments and half-forbidden thoughts.

I believe that there is too much at stake in the reality of these thoughts to keep them hidden. They matter too much for us to say of them, by our behavior, that we have outgrown them or never believed them at all. So far as they are true, they are not fragile unless we neglect them. The only way to test their truth, and the best way to sustain them, is to bring them into the world, to think through them, and to act on them.

For me, writing about these things requires writing about West Virginia. I was born and raised there, on a small hillside farm in the steep, ragged foothills of the Appalachian Mountains. That is where I first knew things that I was sure were real, trustworthy, and mine. It is still the source of my hopes for such things, and my confidence in them. I cannot talk about those things without talking about that place.

My parents came to West Virginia in 1974, the year I was born. They meant to live with few needs, to raise as much of their own food and do as much of their own work as possible, and to share what they could not do themselves with like-minded neighbors. As my father once said to me, they intended "to pick out a small corner of the world and make it as sane as possible." They chose a little more than a hundred acres, mostly steep, eroded pastures and second-growth oak woods, in the uneven bowl of a broad hollow. One side of the hollow was steep and wooded, the other gentler and cleared as meadow. At its back the bowl's lip lowered into a gap between two ridges. At the end of our property the hillsides drew into a narrow passage, where our creek leapt out into a waterfall, and our dirt road clung to the hillside.

Our home is still there, and the land is unchanged;

but I am writing in the past tense. I am writing about how I began.

Our parents taught my younger sister and me at home. Or, rather, it is easiest to say that: we were "homeschoolers." Really, though, our parents did something more radical. They freed us to learn. There were no tests, no lesson plans, no assignments. We made no distinction between the summer and the school year, marked by the appearance of yellow buses on the hard road that we could see below us when we walked a few hundred yards out the dirt driveway. Instead, we played endless games with sticks, pebbles, old clothes, mud that we slathered across our naked bodies, and wildflowers that we arranged in my sister's hair. We worked alongside our parents when we were asked or moved to: we dug potatoes, fed and curry-brushed the Percheron work-horses that my father used for plowing, haying, and logging, and herded our milk and beef cows pasture to pasture. We took part in—or more often were just welcome to listen to—adult conversation as readily as we joined in children's play.

Although we did not precisely study, we read constantly, moving from topic to topic in a steadily expanding landscape of understanding, where each answered question occasioned a dozen, interconnected, further outcroppings of curiosity. If there could have been a map of our learning, it would have resembled nothing so much as a topographic sketch of my many daylong rambles, in which each newly discovered ridge could drop me into five unexplored hollows, and the streams of those hollows lead me to broader valleys, then back to other ridges, so that a picture of a place grew out of years of small, cumulative explorations.

We did not know the distinctions that most people take for granted, and which we have since learned to expect. Between adults and children there were few divisions. I counted old farmers, adult homesteaders like my parents, and other children equally among my friends. Older people addressed us children seriously, and we learned to approach them and one another in the same way. Home and school were as indistinguishable as doing and learning. The home was also the workplace, and the work that we and our parents did was visibly, tangibly devoted to building up and maintaining our place. Home was also the site of community and political life, where meetings took place for our food-buying cooperative, where neighbors gathered around a case of beer to hang the rafters of our timber-frame home in a long evening of daredevil carpentry, and where signs were painted and urgent meetings held when my mother made first a failed, and then a successful run for our county's school board.

Why is it so important that I describe this, my own private West Virginia? Partly, because that experience was an exercise in trust: my parents' trust that their children would want and be able to learn, without classrooms or textbooks and against the warnings of experts; that a marginal place, a small piece of land and an eccentric community, would be full of lessons enough to satisfy two young people; that they, our parents, could get by, learning new kinds of work for a new place and learning them well.

That time was, also, knowing exactly what we relied upon, what we could not do without: the rain that filled our springs or left them too dry for showers and laundry; the sunshine that dried newly cut hay, which a single thunderstorm could ruin; the natural gas, piped from a well on the hollow's steeper slope, that fired our stove and heaters and whose pipes froze on some cold winter nights; the sugar maples that, when there was a freeze by night and a thaw by day, ran with sweet, clear sap that we boiled down to syrup; the steers, which we had named as newborns and watched as they grew, and which we slaughtered and cleaned on cold winter days to put by a year's meat.

In all of these ways, West Virginia meant perfect confidence in the reality of things. I developed one of our hillside springs, digging out a natural seep, filling it with filtering gravel, and ditching out a pipe-run between it and our house, more than a hundred yards below. I drilled the boreholes that brought sap from the living wood of our maples. Although I never pulled the trigger when we slaughtered our steers, I helped to skin and gut a few that I had named. When we spoke about these things, there, we could be confident that our words sat squarely on things that we knew in common.

Maybe because so much of our talk had to do with these stable, certain, solid things, West Virginia was not an ironic place. There was not much talk of trust, hope, or reliance; but there was a great deal of each of those, so thoroughly present that there was no need to name them. They were bound up in the things we did name.

My upbringing was a blend of centuries, with strands of old American idyll and always elements of whatever year the calendar announced. Since leaving that time between times, I have never left behind a sense of betwixtness, of being from somewhere else—another place and, in some measure, another period, another way of living. Wherever I found myself, I came as a visitor, often a willing participant, but never exactly a member. Something in me is always native to another place. But the more I am of these new places and populations, the more imperfectly I am of that anomalous and mainly irretrievable Appalachian childhood.

This is my answer to the question of why, to talk about America today, I first have to say a few things about my upbringing. In some ways, my experience of West Virginia is anomalous. In another way, though, I think that it is typical. We are, many of us, from several places, literally or figuratively. We are shaped by several species of loyalty and aspiration. It is not uncommon for us to find ourselves quietly defending a portion of our past from the demands of our very different present—or drawing on that past, however openly or secretly, to enable us to pass through the present on terms that are partly our own.

More specifically, we nearly all have the sorts of experiences and memories that West Virginia gives me. They reassure us of, or keep us from entirely surrendering, the possibility of trust, of confidence in reality. I do not think that I can write intelligently about these things without naming them, describing them, trying to show the sorts of things that they are. And I cannot do that, with any strength or accuracy, unless I name the things that I have known, and still carry with me.

The burden of this book is twofold. It is that more things than we usually recognize may deserve our trust or hope. It is also that, if we care for certain things, we must in honesty hazard some hope in their defense. A good deal of what we value most, whether openly or in silence, clearly or confusedly, is necessarily common. These are things that affect us all, and we can only preserve or neglect them together. In the end they cannot be had alone.

Defending this idea means resisting the cheapening of words by thoughtless use and by the sophisticated and cynical manipulations of advertising and politics. Those uses make words mere tools for getting what their users want—typically sales, sympathy, or votes. They also corrode our belief that words can have other kinds of power, that they can bring us nearer to things and help us to be more attentive to them.

One response is to try to draw out in words a hope that begins as intensely personal, trusting that another will say, "Yes, you are not alone in that."

This is, perhaps, the work of a love letter, a form that is little practiced today. Such a letter brings something delicate and intimate into the light of shared vision. This disclosure is hazardous and frightening, but it is necessary because the kind of love that moves between people cannot survive in solitude. It must be made common if it is to live at all. Love letters, then, require the courage to stake oneself on an expression of hope that may very well come to nothing. They also indicate a perception of importance, a sense that some possibilities, however unlikely, are so important that not acknowledging them would be an act of terrible neglect.

I have written this book for two reasons: so that I will not forget what I hope for now, and because others might conclude that they hope for the same things. That would be the beginning of turning some of our private, half-secret repositories of hope and trust into common things. I think that some of them must be common, if they are to be at all.

We live in the disappointed aftermath of a politics that aspired to change the human predicament in elemental ways, but whose hopes have resolved into heavy disillusionment. We have difficulty trusting the speech and thought that we might use to try to make sense of our situation. We have left behind an unreal hope to fall into a hopelessness that is inattentive to and mistrustful of reality. What we might hope for now is a culture able to approach its circumstances with attention and care, and a politics that, as part of a broader responsibility for common things, turns careful attention into caring practice.

I mean this book as one invitation to turn our attention to essential and neglected things, and a suggestion about the shape that such renewed attention might take. It is one young man's letter of love for the world's possibilities, written in the hope that others will recognize their own desire in it and will respond. I cannot help believing that we need a way of thinking, and doing, that has in it more promise of goodness than the one we are now following. I want to speak a word for that belief, in the hope of an answer.

For Common Things

Introduction

"TRUST thyself," wrote Ralph Waldo Emerson in "Self-Reliance." "Insist on yourself. Never imitate." For Emerson, the possibility of trusting and insisting on oneself was the promise of America. Throughout history, men and women had bowed before authority and tradition, believing what they were taught, behaving as they were instructed, passing their lives in obedience. Now, he declared, "Whosoever would be a man must be a nonconformist." Each person was obliged to give his own life shape, to achieve by some combination of creation and discovery what Emerson's friend Henry David Thoreau called "an original relation to the universe." America would be something utterly new, Emerson urged: a nation of nonconformists. In relentless originality, "A nation of men shall at last exist, because each believes himself inspired by the Divine Soul which also inspires all men."

Alexis de Tocqueville also believed that Americans represented something new in the world, and that they had Emerson's spirit in them. Every other people in history had moved within hierarchies of authority and deference, privilege and duty. Most people had their place, knew it, and spent their lives trying to fill it competently. In America, though, each white man believed almost instinctively that he was as good, as deserving, as full of possibility as anyone else. Far from knowing his place, the typical American was marked by a deep, hopeful uncertainty about where he might end up—as senator or peddler, prosperous tradesman or skid-row drunk. Wherever he landed, he would get there on his own effort and luck.

Tocqueville saw immediately that Emerson's pronouncements create a paradox: American experience begins not in self-confidence, but in a curious blend of confidence and anxiety that emerges as restlessness. When there is thought to be no good reason that anyone should not be original, the suspicion of unoriginality is widespread and dogging. Where anyone may become rich and powerful, everyone begins to suspect that they are obliged to become rich and powerful. Every life is lived in the shadow of failure—for failure means any ordinary, unremarkable life, and ordinary life casts a large shadow even in a nation of the resolutely extraordinary. If America as a nation was boundlessly hopeful, Americans as individuals were endlessly uneasy.

At the same time, the American faith in equality changed cultural and intellectual life in a basic way: it did away with authority. Any American's opinion was as good as any other's. Like the belief in boundless possibility, the conviction of equal authority had a paradoxical result. Instead of liberating debate about ideas, politics, and the arts, it flattened them and drained them of interest. That everyone's opinion be equally worthwhile might seem from a distance to open up a free-for-all of argument and exploration. Up close, though, it meant that the American was disinclined to take anyone's opinion seriously: Why listen to *him*, talking as though he knew better than anyone else? Rather than burst into a newly egalitarian public life, people were inclined to shut up, close their ears, and turn their attention to something concrete, like making money.

America, then, was characterized by a new kind of movement. In economic life and in the contest for social prestige and political power, the new nation was in constant motion, a hectic, disorderly scramble for goods that were never enough. Yet in culture, in intellectual life, and in serious discussion of public affairs, America was curiously static. There was a kind of psychological inertia, a disbelief that *that* kind of argument was really worth having. America was both constant upheaval and disconcerting stillness.

What do Tocqueville's Americans—these odd, utterly new creatures, the ambivalent portents of Europe's future—have to do with us? I am inclined to say that the answer is: everything. Awash in wealth, we worry that we are required to collect our share. Our idea of success is an almost unworldly prosperity and security, our idea of failure the unextraordinary existence that most of us actually lead. We are constantly in motion, and we can scarcely be satisfied.

Our leading cultural currency today is a version of the stubbornly flat skepticism that Tocqueville observed. We practice a form of irony insistently doubtful of the qualities that would make us take another person seriously: the integrity of personality, sincere motivation, the idea that opinions are more than symptoms of fear or desire. We are wary of hope, because we see little that can support it. Believing in nothing much, especially not in people, is a point of vague pride, and conviction can seem embarrassingly naive.

Finally, our fantasies—the ideas in which we would most like to place our trust, and sometimes bring ourselves to do so—still display Emerson's spirit, though not at its best. We imagine perfect self-sufficiency, the need for no one else in making our lives complete. We still seek an original relation to the universe, although our ways of pursuing that condition are often outlandish and unconvincing. We replace the Divine Soul with other sources of unearned self-confidence, answering a flat and remote cultural world with unworldly conviction in guardian angels and other allies whose existence assures us that the universe is not indifferent to our presence in it.

Our restlessness, our irony, and our fantasies are all elements of a peculiarly American problem: a confused estimation of our powers, our limits, and our needs that has made us indifferent to one of our most indispensable requirements: public life. My hope in this book is to say something illuminating and possibly useful about what we want and what we fear, how our culture weighs on us. I propose that when we retreat from public life, we fall into exaggerated visions of our own powers or dreams of empyreal alliances. I suggest that this retreat is unnecessary and a mistake, and that we can do better for both Emerson's hope and our own very different circumstances.

CHAPTER ONE

Avoiding the World

All things are full of weariness; a man cannot utter it; the eye is not satisfied with seeing, nor the ear filled with hearing. What has been is what will be, and what has been done is what will be done; and there is nothing new under the sun.

—*Ecclesiastes 1:8–9*

CERTAIN personalities bring together the convictions, aspirations, and misgivings that are ambient in an era. Today the attitude that we all encounter and must come to terms with is the ironist's. This is the stance of comedian Jerry Seinfeld, whose departure from the airwaves in 1998 made the front page of the *New York Times*. The end of the show seemed curiously insignificant, not because *Seinfeld* didn't matter, but because the program so perfectly echoed the tone of the culture that its new half-hour each week had triumphed by achieving redundancy. Like William Butler Yeats in W. H. Auden's elegy, Seinfeld became his admirers. There is some of him in all of us.

For he is irony incarnate. Autonomous by virtue of his detachment, disloyal in a manner too vague to be mistaken for treachery, he is matchless in discerning the surfaces whose creature he is. The point of irony is a quiet refusal to believe in the depth of relationships, the sincerity of motivation, or the truth of speech—especially earnest speech. In place of the romantic idea that each of us harbors a true self struggling for expression, the ironist offers the suspicion that we are just quantum selves—all spin, all the way down.

The ironic response to these uncertain currents is eager acquiescence. This distinguishes the ironist from that more somber and familiar beast, the cynic. The cynic, harboring at least a residual sense of his own superiority, stays home and denounces callow and frivolous party-goers. The ironist goes to the party and, while refusing to be quite *of* it, gets off the best line of the evening. An endless joke runs through the culture of irony, not exactly at anyone's expense, but rather at the expense of the idea that anyone might take the whole affair seriously.

Irony does not reign everywhere; it cannot be properly said to reign at all. It is most pronounced among media-savvy young people. The more time one has spent in school, and the more expensive the school, the greater the propensity to irony. This is not least among the reasons that New York and Hollywood, well populated with Ivy League–educated scriptwriters, produce a popular culture drenched in irony. Even where the attitude is most prevalent, most people move between irony and seriousness as they shift from the workplace to their apartments to conversations with parents or romantic partners. Still, the idiom is recognizable everywhere, and it is a rare person under thirty-five who does not participate in it.

The ironic attitude is most pervasive in popular culture, when Karl Marx's dictum that historic events occur twice—"the first time as tragedy, the second as farce"—which had never before been much use except as an insult to alleged second-timers, has found a new vitality. In a movement exemplified by the *Saturday Night Live*–derived movie *Wayne's World*, programmers and screenwriters have turned their own archives into a satiric resource. *Wayne's World* was a pastiche of pop culture, mostly of 1970s vintage, in which heavy metal lyrics blended with stock characters and catchphrases from sitcoms and cartoons. Several years later, MTV presented *Beavis and Butt-head*, a cartoon whose eponymous antiheroes spend their time watching MTV—and subtly mocking its melodramatic, oversexed videos. Now, from comedies to commercials, viewers are invited to join TV programmers in celebrating just how much more clever they are than TV programmers.

Irony is not just something we watch; it is something we do. Although there is nothing so simple as a culture, or even a subculture, of irony, the attitude pervades our thought and behavior. The ironic individual is a bit like Seinfeld without a script: at ease in banter, versed in allusion, and almost debilitatingly self-aware. The implications of his words are always present to him. Like the characters in *Wayne's World*, we find ourselves using phrases that are caught up in webs we did not weave, from their history on *The Brady Bunch* to President Clinton's recent use of them to their role in the latest book of pop spirituality. In our most important moments, we inhabit a cultural echo chamber. The combined effect of ubiquitous television personalities, sanctimonious political pronouncements, and popular spiritualism has been to render cliche nearly anything that anyone would feel it important to say.

Not only our speech, but also our actions and perceptions have undergone the same transformation. We suspect that our feelings, even those we would like to think most intimate, are somehow trite before we express them, sometimes even before we experience them. In romance, we all know picture-perfect courtship from *Love Story*, send-ups of the same suit from satires on romantic comedy, and ironic recastings of the original perfection in which perfection itself is the joke. Walking hand in hand, we cast a shadow before the film projector. Echoing the words of screenwriters and the rhythms of perfume advertisements, we mime a thousand carefully set images of spontaneous delight. We know this, but we cannot escape it.

Even as unique moments come to seem impossible, uniqueness itself has been made trivial. The recent apex of this movement is the proliferation of billboards adorned by Apple Computer with black-and-white, pensive facial shots of anointed geniuses, urging each and every one of us to "think different." The exhortation to imitate genius, which properly names only original, nonderivative, and inimitable thought or creation, would mystify anyone who had not been well prepared to accept it.

We have been so prepared by years of exposure to idealized portrayals of the moments that make each person's life unique in his own thought: falling in love, marrying, making love, reuniting with an estranged father, saying good-bye to an aged grandparent. The aim of these portrayals, in movies, television, and advertisements, is to draw on the power of intimate moments. But the relationship is parasitic. As we become more sophisticated viewers of these portrayals, we also become more sophisticated observers of our own words and acts. Instead of seeing unique significance in the artificial moments of the public world, we begin to doubt the significance of our private words and lives. We can be urged to imitate genius only because we do not quite believe in it. We know too much to think of ourselves, or anybody else, as original or unique.

This is not a conclusion. It is a nagging suspicion, always present to accuse us of triteness in every word or feeling. Faced with a choice between platitude and silence, the ironist in more earnest moments offers strings of disclaimers, sometimes explicit, more often conveyed in gesture or tone, insisting on the inadequacy of her sentences even as she relies on them. In lighter moments she revels in cliche, creating the oft-reported impression that today's youthful conversation is little more than an amalgam of pop-culture references, snatches of old song lyrics, and bursts of laughter at what would otherwise seem the most solemn moments.

Growing Up Ironic

Irony is powered by a suspicion that everything is derivative. It generates a way of passing judgment—or placing bets—on what kinds of hope the world will support. Jerry Seinfeld's stance resists disappointment or failure by refusing to identify strongly with any project, relationship, or aspiration. An ironic attitude to politics and public life never invites disappointment by a movement's decline or a leader's philandering. There is a kind of security here, but it is the negative security of perpetual suspicion.

What do we find so untrustworthy that we dare put such scant weight on it? We surely mistrust our own capacity to bear disappointment. So far as we are ironists, we are determined not to be made suckers. The great fear of the ironist is being caught out having staked a good part of his all on a false hope—personal, political, or both.

Some of this is a reaction against the perceived excesses of the previous generation. People under thirty-five are routinely invited to view their parents' contemporaries as a bit naive, a bit irresponsible, and often blameworthy for those foibles. Douglas Coupland, the author who popularized the term "Generation X," presents his protagonists' parents as clueless at best, wild-eyed and acid-wasted at worst—all victims of an innocence that our ironists are determined

not to revisit. Recent polls showing that college fresh-
men have fewer grand hopes and more commitment
to making money than ever in memory reveal less the
grand avidity of the movie *Wall Street*'s Gordon
Gecko than a suspicion that nothing else is quite
worth the risk.

Some of that suspicion is grounded in the changing
currents of history and culture. One of the defining features of the current generation's experience is
the disappearance of credible public crusades, of the
belief that politics can bring about an elementally different and better world. Instead of inspiration, contemporary irony finds in public life a proliferation of
cant that reinforces ironic skepticism. Emotions have
attracted relentless and often vapid attention in recent
decades, abetted by the confessional culture of talk
shows and choreographed political repentance that
makes such concern unabashedly public. The young
ironist rightly feels that *that* species of sincerity is
more honored in the breach than in the observance.
Today's irony also reacts to a curious conjunction in
public life between the rhetoric of evangelical revival
and the behavior of low vaudeville; Jim and Tammy
Faye Bakker sometimes seem to have formed the mold
for the public figures of the past decade.

A deeper commonality brings both public and private life within the ironic ambit. It is a truism that the
credibility of what we say depends as much on who
we are as on our words themselves. When a person
declares a moral commitment, in order to take him
seriously we must believe that he might lead a life at

least partly oriented by that commitment. Exhortations to chastity don't mean much from a philanderer, nor does praise of patriotism from a quisling. Realizing this, we have long walked a crooked and not entirely fair line between skepticism and obtuseness. The moral authority that John F. Kennedy and Martin Luther King, Jr., exercised rested partly on the public's not knowing the details of their private lives, and most people will grant that ignorance did the country some good.

Somewhere along the line, though, we adopted two ideas that together make it difficult to take anyone's seriousness very seriously. Self-aware in the extreme, we are permeated by Sigmund Freud's view that "we are all ill," that everyone's motivations are in some measure selfish, ignoble, or neurotic. From Shakespeare to James Joyce, good minds have always been able to perceive the base in the trappings of nobility; but more and more, the debunker's language is our vocabulary of first resort. Today's young people are adept with phrases that reduce personality to symptoms, among them "passive-aggressive," "repressed," and "depressive." It is revealing that anyone who regards his own standards a little too reverently is likely to be labeled not proud—hardly a compliment for most of our history—but "anal." We all have it in the back of our minds that our behavior is subject to psychologizing interpretation, and that we, creatures of multiple and obscure motives that we are, cannot protest our integrity in response.

This idea has combined with a mainly unspoken

presumption that "values" are not unchanging, impersonal standards. Instead they are intensely personal guideposts, selected because they help us to shape our lives at particular times, then replaced as we grow and move on. This is surely one of the reasons that divorce has become so frequent and accepted, and it is one that many see cause to acknowledge, if not exactly to celebrate. We are more inclined than ever before to say that "people's values change," and that new projects discovered in midlife may carry people onto irreconcilable paths. According to this view, professing a value does not so much acknowledge an objective commandment as say something about the shape one has given one's own life.

It is now common even to hear religion discussed in these terms. If there is a meaningful distinction between religion and the fashionably vague "spirituality," it is that the shape and content of spirituality are almost exclusively personal. All of this means that "values" describe more than they prescribe. Just as economists take our choices to be "preference-revealing," showing what we really want, so we more and more take our actions to reveal what we really value.

In this climate, someone who professes loyalty to a principle is perceived to be expressing his own character, not describing the strictures that he is subject to as a Christian, a Jew, or just (his view of) a human being. When a gap develops between his expression and his behavior, he is not just another fallen creature or "all too human," but a hypocrite. Hypocrisy,

unlike other flaws, can be resolved by redefinition—
by professing a set of values closer to one's actions. So
we increasingly take high principle to be a source of
unnecessary discomfort or unearned self-importance,
rather than an acknowledgment that we are called to
be better than we are. We are all ill, and to aspire to
wellness is to invite debunking. Our being human
has become a strong argument against cleaving to
demanding values, or respecting them in others. In a
curious way, we consider ourselves too honest for
that.

One ironic response to all this skepticism concludes that, if surfaces are all we have to work with,
we had better make our surfaces as compelling as
possible. Management guru Tom Peters urges the
young and ambitious to "brand" themselves, to shape
others' perceptions to their own advantage just as
they would market a new product. "We are," Peters
writes, "CEOs of our own companies: Me, Inc. To
be in business today, our most important job is to be
head marketer for the brand called You." Marketing
becomes a form of life.

Peters's doctrine chimes unsettlingly with a widespread suspicion that marketing is not a bad metaphor for what most of us do most of the time. An
inevitable consequence of sophistication about the
received significance of words, tones, and gestures is
keen awareness of self-presentation as a production.
This sophistication adds a new edge to the old question, "What does she mean by that?" The answer will
seldom appear at face value. From the utterly self-

conscious conventionalism of the book of strategic dating etiquette *The Rules* to the contrived anti-conventionalism of shock-jock celebrities and their imitators, we have reason to be less attentive to what people say and do than to what they might be trying to get by it. When speech and action are marketing, what they reveal is not personality but ambition, not an individual one could know, but a bundle of aims and desires that may or may not coincide with one's own.

Yet just as we are too savvy to take commercials seriously, so we can take only a wary pleasure in people whom we know to be peddling themselves, and whose campaigns may shift with their target audience. For all its ready laughter, the ironic mood is secretly sad. Tom Peters has rather grand predecessors, notably Oscar Wilde, who declared, "The first duty in life is to be as artificial as possible. What the second duty is no one has yet discovered." But Wilde drew from wells that are now mostly dry. Despite his talk of artificiality, he was in some measure a romantic who believed that he displayed his true identity by flouting convention; he was not exactly a quantum self. Moreover, his eccentricities had the charge and thrill of dramatic dissent in a conventional era. Now, the fashions of dissent are on sale at specialty boutiques, and between the prematernal Madonna and the merrily depraved cartoon *South Park* there is less and less left in convention whose flouting can elicit shock.

The ironic stance invites us to be self-absorbed,

but in selves that we cannot believe to be especially interesting or significant. Its sophistication is sapping, a way of cultivating suspicion of ourselves and others. Refusing to place its trust in the world, irony helps to make a world that is the more likely to be worthy of despair. And so, despite our assiduous efforts to defend ourselves from it, disappointment and a quiet, pervasive sadness have crept into our lives.

The Hunger for Home

Irony is only half of a picture with two symmetrical portions. In the ironic view, each individual is essentially alone. The superficiality of relationships and the ambivalent obligation to "brand" one's own personality set up sharp and mainly insurmountable differences among people. At the same time, the ironic reluctance to identify with a larger ambition—say, a political party or a community project—means that the ironist does not have the reassuring experience of finding his own commitments reaffirmed by others. A partisan, or just a partner, takes sustenance from relationships that are shaped by a common project and infused with the values that underlie the project. Some sorts of religious believers and political devotees even find their convictions reinforced as they perceive God's plan or the Progress of History fulfilling itself in the world around them. In all of these experiences there is an intimacy with one's setting, a sense of being connected rather than alone, consonant rather than idiosyncratic. The ironist has none of this.

Partly in response to that privation, our age of irony is also an age of belief—ambivalent, often frustrated belief, which bears the marks of its ironic competitor, but belief nonetheless. Even in the midst of irony, there is a widespread hunger to feel oneself made whole, connected with true values that are also the values of one's community and, in some cases, of the world itself.

Thus we inhabit a culture in which *Seinfeld*'s popularity was recently rivaled by the second-ranked television drama, *Touched by an Angel,* part of a flood of material on the benign, winged creatures. The contemporary angel is not the agent of a jealous or even particularly zealous God, but is rather a kind of therapist-cum-advocate and celestial valet. Bestiaries and user's guides have crowded onto best-seller lists in the 1990s, among them Sophy Burnham's *A Book of Angels* and Karen Goldman's *Angel Voices.* In 1994, the *New York Times* best-seller list included eight books on the topic at various times. According to these accounts, angels not only help us to keep our emotions steady, make sound judgments about relationships, and advance our careers, but also provide small incidents of divine intervention, often on the order of retrieving lost keys or starting a recalcitrant engine. Angels, that is, tell us that the universe is not indifferent to our existence.

The meaningfulness of things is fundamental to a tradition that begins on the one hand in Plato's and Aristotle's discourses on the intelligibility of reality, on the other in the declaration that "In the beginning was the Word." We are inheritors of the idea that intelligence and at least partly comprehensible order lie at the root of all that is. However, the experience of the past hundred-odd years has been marked by the growth of the idea that the world's order can neither guide nor nurture us, that any significance it may have is essentially inhuman. In the phrase of the German thinker Max Weber, the world has become "disenchanted."

Perhaps the greatest evocation of this experience comes from the nineteenth-century English poet Matthew Arnold, who in "Dover Beach" describes the withdrawal of "the Sea of Faith." As it passes, there remains before him only "Its melancholy, long, withdrawing roar, / Retreating, to the breath / Of the night wind, down the vast edges drear / And naked shingles of the world." The naked world is, we insistently feel, not ours. We are native to a world clothed in moral significance, one in which our aspirations are recognized and our hopes, whether fulfilled or not, at least registered, recognized, understood. But now, the world naked, deaf, and mute often seems all that remains to us.

Angels answer this awful apprehension. Ministering to our sadness and loneliness, they assure us that we are not unloved. Our feelings matter to another being—our guardian angel—as much as they do to us. By interceding in the course of events, angels propose that this celestial concern is not subjective—not just the kind of sympathy that another person might feel for us—but tied up with the natural processes that stall an engine or carry a dropped key through a grate. In other words, the very fabric of things can respond to our desires, even our small and transient ones. If the world does not revolve around us, it does at least wobble our way on occasion. Angels tell us that it is all right to do just what the ironist will not: place the gambler's burden of hope on the world.

Irony, it must be said, raises the bar for anyone who would maintain conviction. The belief in angels, indeed the whole mass of loose-knit spirituality, only partly clears that bar. By and large, "belief" in these things is really a diffuse hope; few people believe in angels, at least of the popular variety, with the confidence of a true religious believer, let alone the belief of a scientist who trusts in the reliable behavior of chemical reactions. Instead, belief of this sort is an on-again, off-again affair, a way of giving cosmological significance to pleasing events and good luck, and a source of some comfort in misfortune.

In all of these ways, obsession with angels is a peculiarly expansive form of self-involvement, the apotheosis of psychic needs. Angels not only minister to us as isolated, needy bundles of wishes and fears, but paradoxically help us to stay that way. They provide a species of reassurance that we can have alone, in the privacy of our apartments and offices. Being at home in the world does not have to mean changing or reaching beyond ourselves, adjusting our habits and desires to our places and communities; instead, the world answers our wishes, just because they are ours.

Angelic spirituality is also a way of defying the

weariness of an ironic culture. By announcing their hope with an almost pointed naivete, the new spiritualists take a stand against ironic skepticism. It is worth noting, however trivial it may seem, that the same cars whose bumpers announce "Magic Happens" are likely to sport the slogan "Mean People Suck." On their face, the first is metaphysical, the second attitudinal. On closer inspection, both are mainly attitudes. Together they form what might be called the anti-Seinfeld position.

The same hope for a responsive universe, attuned to something other than physical fact, appears in the new, syncretic spiritualism of figures such as Thomas Moore and works like the ostensibly "scribed," or channeled, *A Course in Miracles*. Even the titles of their prominent works present a rebuke to the relentless banality of the ironist. *A Course in Miracles* declares above all that there are such things, that our tired world regularly admits the magical. Moore's *Re-Enchantment of Everyday Life* makes exactly the same proposal: a sense that some things are sacred, and hold a special moral meaning in contrast to merely worldly things, is still available to us; the prefix that begins the book's title, though, accepts that the sacred has been lost, or at least obscured, and must be won back. Similarly, Moore's *Care of the Soul*, the first in a slew of popular uses of a word that for many years was scarcely whispered in the culture of network TV and respectable publishing, declares foremost that we *have* souls, that we are not quantum selves.

Here again, notably in the *Course*'s idiosyncratic borrowing from Christian and other traditions—for instance, keeping salvation while jettisoning sin, which raises the question of what exactly we need to be saved from—spirituality is a matter of reassurance. Its sources are emotional need, and its standards and aims are therapeutic. It consoles more than it challenges, and offers much more than it demands. It is a great comfort. On the whole, it, too, can be had alone.

These are the conflicting moods of the time. We are skeptical, ironic, and inclined to an impoverished self-reliance. At the same time, we want to give up the ironist's jaded independence and believe that we are not alone, that we can find moral communities, clear obligations, and even miracles. We doubt the possibility of being at home in the world, yet we desire that home above all else. We are certain only of ourselves—if in a somewhat precarious way—and we work toward the certainty of something larger. We are fragmentary, even masters of fragmentation, and we hunger for wholeness.

The Fast Lane Home

There is another, more heroic attempt to cross the barriers that irony sets against belief. One way of grasping irony's significance is to consider that the ironic attitude pronounces the impossibility of achieving Thoreau's "original relation to the universe." Where wishing for angels means lightly retouching the world to make it more responsive to our putative originality, the heroic attitude calls on individuals to rework themselves radically enough to become original again. Today this aim finds expression mainly in the walks of life that are widely perceived as the most dynamic, the most transformatory, and the most likely to produce heroes. They are, intriguingly, realms that a few decades ago seemed positively banal: the business world and information technology. Their defining vehicles are a pair of lifestyle magazines, *Fast Company* and *Wired*.

The interest of these magazines is that they speak to a pair of transformations that other media have approached with an obtuseness verging on physical inaptitude. Changes in technology have left the childhood educations of young adults already obsolete, while changes in the economy make their prospects, even if heady, basically uncertain. Today the future consumes the past at an unprecedented rate, and the present provides no stable place to stand. *Fast Company* and *Wired* promise an understanding of the quaking landscape and perhaps even a place to live in it. Their appeal to puzzlement, more than their pretense to heroics, is the key to their attraction. Their failure is that they answer an unsettling reality with unsatisfying fantasy.

Fast Company, the leading vehicle of the businessperson-as-hero idea, is one of the most successful of the wave of start-up magazines from recent years. *Fast Company* presents business as a way of life that leaves behind the prosaic stuff of ordinary existence.

The magazine's refrain is the idea of "free agency": the contemporary economy has cut people loose from traditional, lifelong corporate jobs and spun each of us centrifugally into total freedom and self-reliance. Now everyone is a freelancer.

Fast Company styles the mercenary life a good one. Free agency is not an eviction, but an escape from the constraints of traditional careers, into a new ideal of self-creation as a profit-making exercise. The magazine's definitive discussion of free agency includes the declaration "I declare my independence" from the bonds of job, place, and nation. "Companies do not exist. Countries do not exist. Boundaries are an illusion." Everything that keeps us where we are, weary, flat, and dull, is whisked away as if by the power of a wish. Freedom is born in the pronouncement of freedom.

However, the essential movement of *Fast Company* is less departure than homecoming. The magazine rebels rhetorically against a stereotyped "corporate culture," one of the constraints that the Free Agent is most eager to escape. The villains of its pages are "toxic companies," where bosses are overbearing, employees are alienated, and creativity is stifled. As a representative Free Agent recalls of attending large companies' recruiting sessions: "They were fake, they were plastic." In contrast to all that, "She was looking for authenticity."

"Fake" and "plastic" are conventional ways of abhorring the patina of convention, the all-encompassing triteness that dogs the ironist. They capture the sense that everyone is pretending—and rather inelegantly, at that—to fill out roles that no one can really believe in. Against this, *authenticity* is the real selling point of free agency. This complicated and elusive idea is essential to the "original relation to the universe": we want not just something new, but something that is really *us*. The problem with a world where everything is derivative is the suspicion that we are patched-together remnants of someone else's imagination, unreal, not our own. That is what makes us fear that we are farce rather than tragedy.

The fear of losing authenticity is an old one. The wish for clarity about what we are and are not, a decisive repudiation of artificiality, is Thoreau's hope on going to the woods "to live deliberately, to front only the essential facts of life . . . and not, when I came to die, discover that I had not lived at all." It is the source of Hamlet's fear that, as self-doubt stays his determination from becoming action, he fades into a living ghost before the world. To express oneself whole and unadulterated is the aspiration of a long line of dissenters from convention, from Percy Bysshe Shelley's Romantics and the Surrealists to stream-of-consciousness beat poets.

What is new is that the latest seekers after authenticity are not bohemians, but boardroom Romantics. The spreadsheet has replaced the canvas, the stanza, and the journal. For the first time, the way out of convention is by the superior command of conventional achievements. The way home is through the home office.

The businessperson is an artist, a genius by turns solitary and collaborative. Accordingly, *Fast Company*'s next-favorite fetish after authenticity is "creativity." The magazine's regular "Unit of One" feature, offering quick lessons from exemplary Free Agents, devotes more than a third of its profiles to this idea. The profiled entrepreneurs offer such slogans as "The key to creativity is clarity," "You can't force-feed creativity," "Creativity is a two-step process," and, with a symmetry that is almost elegant, "There's no creativity without authenticity." Art is good, business is art, and there is no good business without art.

Business is also a domesticated form of political commitment. A delighted profile of Chinese entrepreneur Li Lu, who confronted the Beijing regime's tanks at Tiananmen Square in 1989, details his discovery that "business has become the ultimate expression of individuality." "The spirit of Tiananmen," *Fast Company* proclaims, has moved from the streets to the offices of a new breed of Chinese Free Agent. In the less dramatic politics of the United States, the magazine casts a rare approving glance at Mayor John Norquist of Minneapolis because "He certainly doesn't sound like a politician—least of all, like a Democrat. When John Norquist talks, he sounds exactly like a change agent." In the same spirit, tucked between an item on the virtues of bourbon and another on low-cost PCs, is a piece praising an innovative judge as a "Change Agent in a Black Robe." Change agents are the storm troopers of creativity and authenticity, the innovative entrepreneurs and management consultants who make over companies and careers. Politics, in short, is worth attention when it most resembles the heroic version of business. Nothing less can hold the Free Agent's capricious attention.

Thus the artistic heroism of authenticity and the political heroism of declaring principles in the face of power both belong to the business world. This is an extraordinary coup, like Microsoft purchasing Liberty Hall, the Louvre, and perhaps the Vatican. However, it is hardly credible. Business, after all, is neither art nor politics, but only itself. Nor is it a way of remaking oneself, of achieving the elusive original relation to the universe.

Attempts to achieve those aims through money-making and marketing fall back into the unhappy muddle of irony. One of *Fast Company*'s heroes is the same Tom Peters who urges each of us to become something called "brand You." Peters informed readers in a cover article in 1998, "You're every bit as much a brand as Nike, Coke, Pepsi, or the Body Shop. . . . When you're promoting brand You, everything you do—and everything you choose not to do—communicates the value and character of the brand." In other words, life is a hustle.

A hustle, though, is no way to authenticity. With this move we are back to irony, to contrivance, manipulation, and thinness of personality. Surely brand You is no less suspect than the derivative words and phrases that first make the ironist suspect that everything might be more or less reluctant marketing.

Yet *Fast Company* manages to be altogether cheerful about this difficulty, overcoming the distastefulness of the hustle by omitting to notice that it is hustling at all. The implausible interconnectedness of art, politics, business, and authenticity is presented with a smile that is much more naive than knowing. The effort is well intended and delivered with enthusiasm. For all that, though, it is not believable.

This implausibility is not incidental; it is tied up with the fantastic character of the whole *Fast Company* scheme. The magazine offers a vision of being at home in the world while being essentially uprooted: the Free Agent is bound nowhere, but is at ease everywhere. He is comfortable because he is creative and authentic wherever he goes. His creativity shows itself in "working smarter" and "playing the game differently," his authenticity in "strong values." These, though, are not a personality or a form of life; they are catchphrases, like "change agent," notable for signifying nothing in particular. They are phrases that substitute for thought.

The Free Agent is advertised as being in harmony with what is best in the world: he is creation, change, and truthfulness. But in fact, as described in his own lifestyle magazine, he is a strikingly thin creature. There is little sense of what his "strong values" are, of *how* he "plays the game," let alone why he chose to play this particular game rather than any other, or no game at all. What he means by *creativity* and *authenticity* is obscure, and probably could not survive clarity. His rebellion is not a movement, not even a statement, but a gesture. He is the fifteen-second clip of personal contentment that one sees in a nonironic commercial. He is, in other words, brand You.

Fast Company ends by being unconvincing because its fantasy is vague, diffuse, made up mainly of gauzy images and pleasant sounds. The Free Agent, though, has more exotic cousins whose fantasies are more adamant. The most outlandish of these is the tribe of the Digerati, the elite of the new information economy celebrated by *Wired* magazine. *Wired,* which a few years ago enjoyed the kind of launch that has hurried *Fast Company* into prominence, tries to do for computer technology what the younger magazine does for business: make it into a way of life that saves its participants from banality. The magazine's first issue announced, "*Wired* is about the most powerful people on the planet today—the Digital Generation." Despite that grand claim, its most tantalizing promise is not that its lionized audience will rule the world, but that the Digerati, like the Free Agent, can approach the world originally.

Where *Fast Company* follows tepidly in the steps of the Romantics, *Wired* inherits a cartoonish version of the thought of Friedrich Nietzsche, the nineteenth-century German iconoclast whose ideas have become a touchstone for generations of rebels against received morality. Nietzsche believed, like many of our contemporaries, that all myths, magic, and certainty had gone out of the world. The progress of science and rational skepticism had exhausted the plausibility of Europe's great religious tradition, Christianity, and its secular avatar, liberal democracy. This process, what Weber would later call disenchantment, was psychologically devastating, but it also presented a heady opportunity. Christianity and democracy had thrived on repression, training the strong, intelligent, and beautiful in the enervating habits of humility, self-reproach, and egalitarianism. This was a painful distortion of the higher human capacities, the power of free expression and, above all, the power to create liberating, sustaining, and strengthening myths. The end of religious belief meant a new freedom for these powers. Those who possessed strong enough imagination, will, and intellect could celebrate their new liberty in freely chosen communities of similarly extraordinary individuals.

Wired adds a twist to this idea. For the magazine, the key to realizing Nietzsche's promise is technology. "No ambition, however extravagant, no fantasy, however outlandish, can any longer be dismissed as crazy or impossible. This is the age when you can finally do it all. . . . Suddenly technology has given us powers with which we can manipulate not only external reality—the physical world—but also, and much more portentously, ourselves. You can become whatever you want to be." The bold invitation stretches across the first few pages of one issue of the magazine, emblazoned over a computer-generated, Daliesque landscape populated by transparent human forms

whose brains, muscles, and entrails are tangles of silicon chips and fiber-optic cable. The phrases echo one
of *Wired* editor Kevin Kelly's favorite slogans, "We
are as gods, and we might as well get good at it."

The magazine's writers revel in fantastic descrip-
tions of expensive biological and electronic advances
that offer people the capacity to remake themselves.
One set of recurring *Wired* heroes is the Extropians,
a kind of freewheeling cult committed to becoming
supermen through technology. They espouse "a philosophy of freedom from limitations of any kind." On
the Extropians' account, those who can afford it will
eventually be able to overcome mortality by "down-
loading" consciousness into computers, where they
will survive forever as disembodied mind, perhaps
helped along by robotic accessories and virtual-reality
experiences. They are equally committed to pharma-
ceutical, surgical, and other ways of concentrating
and expanding the powers of the mind.

The self-invention that *Wired* imagines is not,
though, completely individual. Instead, the magazine
invites its readers to mark themselves as members of
a tribe, or several tribes, in which an original relation
to the world becomes possible.

In this spirit, *Wired* adopts a digital-pagan tone.
A 1996 cover story celebrated Burning Man, a week-
end gathering in the Nevada desert where high technology and counterculture meet in a festival of body
paint, drumming, and electronically enhanced may-
hem, culminating in the burning of a huge human
figure, a custom adopted from Europe's ancient Celts.

The magazine has adopted as its muse the late Marshall McLuhan, prophet of technological tribalism. In an admiring interview with the successor to McLuhan's professorial chair, Derrick de Kerckhove, *Wired* reports his conviction that Internet users have reattained "a tribal world, [where] the cosmos has a presence. It's alive. The tribe shares in this huge, organic reality." If there is no magic in even the oddest corners of the merely physical world, there can be magic in the artificial worlds of computer-generated virtual reality. There, invented selves can play in invented fields, cultivating an original relation to a thoroughly original universe.

Still, the way to that originality is essentially a consumer's. From the beginning, regular features have announced which ideas and products are "wired" and which "tired"; kept up a "jargon watch"; pointed out the gear and style that bring "street cred," as in credibility; and held forth on "fetishes," the super-products of the super-wired. The magazine's wired/tired and "fetish" features describe the latest symbols of tribal membership, which require constant updating. This tribe is all about being on the move, and about buying. The magazine's ideal reader, when something looks good to him, will do it, buy it, create it, or become it without delay. The Digerati seek comradeship among perceived equals in self-invention and world-making; rather than scorn the less exalted, they are likely to forget their existence altogether. This is an adolescent doctrine, a wish for a fantasy shopping trip without end.

Yet at the same time there is something plaintive in *Wired*, a disappointment in the dull business of the world, the sense of ennui that occasions irony. In place of pabulum and tedium, the magazine offers its readers a glimpse of real community—life in the tribe, where everyone is clever like you, enthusiastic about the same things that delight you, and looking for the same kind of good time that you're after. Kelly's cosmological musings even provide a quasi-religious sense of the meaning of computer work—nature worship rendered in silicon.

What the Digerati have in common with the Free Agent is that, by and large, neither exists. The magazines' readers are not mainly Free Agents, let alone aspiring Extropians. They are curious, concerned about shaping their futures and understanding the present. As angel-watching involves more attitude than metaphysics, so this readership bears more puzzlement than the conviction and self-congratulation that pervade the magazines' tone. *Fast Company*, although a more serious affair than *Wired*, describes the real lives of very few people. We do not, really, ever declare and keep our independence. In the end, we would not wish to. *Wired*, meanwhile, is a testament to the power of artfully rendered fantasy to distract its participants from reality. The magazine's icons are men and women who can take fantasy in full seriousness—at the cost of being taken seriously themselves.

The Digerati and the Free Agent express the poverty of our resources for thinking of our lives as guided by some purpose, filled by some power, or touched by some loveliness outside what we have learned to call banality. Their eminent unreality bespeaks a weakly held hope for the potency of fantasy. Whether in virtual communities or in self-marketing authenticity, we would like to compose stories about ourselves and see those stories come true. We are looking for words and ways of living that will help us make sense of an increasingly complex and elusive world.

We do not especially want the irony that sometimes seems our lot, and do not find the wholeness that we continue to desire. Our attempts to resolve the dilemma seem to draw on the worst in us. It is little wonder that many of us settle into irony as mildly discontented residents, or into one of the competing versions of wholeness as secretly half-doubting partisans. Our fantasies do not hold together, and reality does not hold us. Of the things that we do try to believe in, moreover, politics is no longer one. It is worthwhile to ask why this should be so.

CHAPTER TWO

The Absence of Politics

In democracies there comes about an odious mingling
of the conceptions of baseness and power, of unwor-
thiness and success, and of profit and dishonor.

—*Alexis de Tocqueville,* Democracy in America

POLITICS is undignified, disreputable, vaguely
ridiculous, and thoroughly outmoded. The great
achievements of the age belong to the business world,
its great pleasures to personal relationships and self-
cultivation. Politics is left to tedious, futile crusaders,
overgrown children with insatiable egos, and dubious
bands of hangers-on. It creates nothing useful, beautiful, or profitable. As Auden wrote of poetry, it makes
nothing happen. The appropriate attitude to it is
indifference.

This is the unhappy reputation that politics has
developed in recent decades. Such skepticism is especially pronounced among the youngest adults, men
and women just finishing college or taking their first
jobs. The most idealistic, the ones certain that they
will serve others, seek their work mainly outside government, almost wholly outside the besmirched fields

of campaigns and elections, and mostly not even in the "official" world of Washington advocacy groups. Instead, they choose direct service in housing projects and rural community centers, inner-city schools and Third World villages. Increasingly, they cut a path through the private economy, training as management consultants or lawyers, then turning their skills, wealth, and professional connections toward service. These private-public entrepreneurs are behind much of the explosion in nonprofit service groups and what are pointedly called nongovernmental organizations (NGOs), where much good work now begins. And if the idealists are nongovernmental, the majority is entirely committed to the private economy, where fortunes await those who are adept at maneuvering other people's money and information.

There is truth behind the skepticism. Politics has not acquitted itself well in recent years. No casual observer can miss the widespread venality and intermittent absurdity of politicians. The sexual imbroglios, petty wars of personality, incessant money-grubbing, and theatrical self-righteousness that color national politics need no rehearsal. Yet the problem is not just that our current electoral cast features an exceptional number of buffoons, shallow hypocrites, and bundles of undisciplined appetite. Instead, alongside a sense of the absurdity of politics there has developed a general perception of its futility. The same government that, thirty-five years ago, could launch a "war on poverty" with considerable support and spearhead real progress toward racial equality is now decisive only in dismantling its own previous initiatives. As to what government ought to do, there is a distinct lack of resonant proposals. In the absence of inspiring programs, the best in politics have little to do—little even to hold them there—while the worst have no distractions from their burlesque performance. There is always garbage in government; it is constantly on the surface when the political waters are otherwise stagnant.

For all that, the turn away from politics is not just a response to what public life has become. Instead, both the indifference to politics and, in lesser measure, its stagnation are symptoms of a lack in the culture. One thing that a culture does is to give people ways of thinking about what they are doing. They can see the connections among their work, their talents, and the needs of the world. They perceive their work as belonging to a whole, some of whose possibilities are good, which they help to sustain.

In other words, a rich culture helps people to say what their work is for, what its purposes are. This means that an architect can understand how her work serves the purpose of creating heartening places for people to live and work, a journalist the aim of informing people of their community's business and the world's, a doctor making possible healthy lives, or a farmer feeding people and maintaining fertile land. A person can also appreciate how her trade enhances her own life by developing her best talents or important human qualities: for the architect, spatial and aesthetic perception and an intuitive sense of how space either puts people at ease or disquiets them; for the journalist, effective writing, a feeling for the line between truth and falsehood, and the knack for drawing scattered facts into an intelligible story. Moreover, a culture presents us with standards of excellence that are independent of us and dignify our work when we satisfy them: sound and gracious design, clear and true writing, or the health of a farmer's fields and livestock.

Work that can be good in these elemental ways can also, necessarily, be bad. It can fail. There are ruined fields, unintelligible essays, and displeasing buildings. Just as good work gives a measure of sense and dignity to a person's activity, bad work is degrading. A job or an industry that does not offer the possibility of good work, that is manifestly unnecessary, that develops no talents, that achieves no excellences, is a species of tragedy, or of insult.

There are such industries, and there are people who do potentially good work shoddily or indifferently. Even people who work very well do not spend much time pondering the ways that their work is good work. Still, these qualities—purpose, self-cultivation, and excellence—are present in the background of day-to-day work, and many people can be quietly aware of the ways in which their trades are worthwhile. These benefits are subtle, but they are sustaining.

Today we have no such way of understanding politics. However we approach it, we find a low, disheartening occupation, one that even at its best is narrow and parochial. We can hardly say what good politics is: how it serves others, how it enhances its practitioners, or what standards of excellence it could hope to meet. To each of these questions we respond with something between uncertainty and resignation. We cannot, in effect, say what politics is for.

What Politics Is Now

To talk about politics today is to presume insincerity. It is the first requirement of even modest political sophistication to understand that public figures neither say what they mean nor mean what they say. Rather than expressions of conviction, public statements are moves made according to the shifting rules of an elaborate game. The thing to understand is not what is said, but the goal that the speaker is manipulating us to achieve. No one imagines that the congressional Republicans who opposed campaign finance reform in 1997 and 1998 did so out of concern for the status of the First Amendment, no matter how adamant their protestations; everyone knows that incumbents' first concern is to keep their seats. Many people disbelieved Bill Clinton's initial denial of an affair with a White House intern in 1998; yet many of the same people accepted that the president claimed what he had to claim, under the circumstances, in order to hold on to the presidency. In the same scandal, Hillary Rodham Clinton's outspoken denunciation of her husband's accusers was analyzed in terms of "the White House defense strategy," not as the expression of a wife's conviction. In the Clinton administration's better times, the fact that the president's proposals in domestic policy were a wind sock in the shifting breezes of the polls stirred no surprise; after all, such proposals are made, by and large, for political advantage. Someone who asked more of a politician would reveal that she misunderstood the rules of the game.

When politics is regarded as a self-serving variety of theater, it should come as no surprise that it assumes the cast of entertainment. The most prevalent attitude toward politics after indifference treats it as a hybrid of spectator sport and *People* magazine's celebrity culture. The Sunday-morning talk shows are fodder for the sports-fan stance, providing competing accounts of who's up, who's down, and what the smart money is on during the coming week. The magazine *George* is the centerpiece of the celebrity-culture view of politics, hanging on personalities, relationships, career trajectories, and gossip in a way that helped to earn Washington the sardonic description "Hollywood for ugly people."

Except for exciting those who participate in political fandom, this understanding of politics encourages general indifference. For most people, especially young adults contemplating careers, the view of politics as self-serving theater is uninspiring. It promises a career of manipulating other people, cynically adjusting and misrepresenting one's convictions, and, maybe, achieving a minor species of notoriety. This is unsatisfying not only to the high motivation of honor, but also to the middling one of ordinary dignity. This is how we describe politics to ourselves, how we regard it when we consider the kinds of work that we might take up. It is little wonder, then, that most of us are disinclined to undertake it.

Politics today comes across as not only a low business, but also a parochial one. A politician's goal in life appears to be just this: to remain a politician. Political activity is not foremost motivated by things outside itself. Instead, it aims at its own kind of success, electoral victory and ascent within a party or government, and is satisfied with that. The rest is incidental. Politicians respond to public concerns when political success requires that response, but the politician is just as happy to enjoy an undemanding constituency that will reliably reelect him every few years.

Here again, politics is like sport: a game you can observe if you wish, but which will not miss you if you choose not to cheer, and whose end-of-season standings matter mainly to its participants and their loyal fans. Filled with this perception, citizens, and especially young people, are inclined to view politics as someone else's game, unimportant to those who have more pressing business. The game of politics seems hardly to touch the ordinary lives that most concern most of us.

In the Absence of Politics

One reason for the hollow echo that we find in politics now is the eclipse of what might be called Promethean ambitions. I take the term from Prometheus, the figure of Greek legend who stole fire from the gods in order to give it to humanity, and so changed the human world forever. His bold act—for which he was punished with an eternity of torment—is the great emblem of a rebellion against what *is* in favor of what might be, of staking oneself on the possibility of transforming the human condition.

One of the vivid promises of public life in recent centuries has been that politics might bring about basic changes in the human predicament. This means not only improving institutions or alleviating ills, but actually eliminating certain elemental problems. With this aim the political impulse takes on a special power as great as the plagues that politics promises to dissolve. That heady promise has recently seemed to disappear, and we are deeply affected by its passing.

The first great instance of this political ambition emerged in the work of the eighteenth-century French philosopher Jean-Jacques Rousseau. A provincial who made his way to the court of Versailles and the high culture of Paris, Rousseau was disgusted by the flattery, sycophancy, and condescension that he saw around him. He viewed these as the sickly sweet fruits of sophistication, the consequences of the desire for respect and recognition, a desire that comes with distinctions in social rank and afflicts people more acutely as they become more self-conscious and worldly. The low flatter the high, the high despise the low yet would not forgo their flattery, and no one can rest easy with himself. When he famously wrote "Man is born free, but everywhere he is in chains,"

Rousseau meant these fetters of the mind as much as any.

Rousseau proposed that these psychic agonies might be overcome through politics. His theory of the social contract describes the conditions necessary for everyone to enjoy equal respect among his fellows. By creating a civic realm in which every citizen is absolutely equal to every other, and making this the primary site of moral identification, politics brings us what we most need: every man has the regard of every other, which he earnestly reciprocates.

Because so much is at stake in the unity of the political community, it must not be divided against itself. Accordingly, once the community is founded by each member's relinquishment of his private will and interests to the authority of the whole, all must obey the "general will," or common interest, in whose name political authority operates. Those who resist "must be forced to be free." If they were permitted their resistance, they would split the community, and the great moral achievement of politics would be undone.

Rousseau's general will is less democratic than an expression of a semimystical bond among citizens, and there are no intrinsic limits on what force it can apply to preserve "freedom." In promising to change the human condition, politics assumes a new authority over other areas of life and over the will of any particular individual. In other words, the theories of political liberation and of totalitarianism are born here at the same moment. Because it addresses certain of our supreme needs and hopes, politics attains a supremacy of its own.

The most ambitious program of Promethean politics came in the Marxist tradition of communist revolution. Marx's central idea—which in adulterated form became the governing ideology of the Soviet Union and its European colonies, China and much of Southeast Asia, Cuba, and a generation of Latin American and African revolutionaries—was simple and dramatic. The most important thing about us, Marx suggested, is our work. Work makes us who we are. Understand what a person does, and under what conditions he does it, and you will have understood him. See how a society organizes its work, and you will see through to its core.

Marx's ideal was free labor. He looked forward to a world where each person could choose his own work, day by day or hour by hour if he wished, and so "hunt in the morning, fish in the afternoon, rear cattle in the evening, criticise after dinner, without ever becoming hunter, fisherman, shepherd or critic." This would mean a world of free self-creation: in selecting your work, you would decide the *sort of person* you wished to be, the skills you would develop, and the goods you would produce and identify as your own. Then, at the call of a whim, you would set that work aside and take up something new in an improvisational dance of choice and labor.

What Marx saw around him, as he wrote in nineteenth-century proto-Germany and Britain, was a systematic violation of this ideal, where workers took whatever jobs would keep them in food and shelter, and even capitalists were the slaves of the balance sheet, always driven by the threat of bankruptcy. Neither the exploited laborers nor their exploiters had real freedom in choosing how they spent their hours and energies. An economic and social analyst more than a political thinker, Marx believed that capitalism's periodic crises would shake it apart, permitting workers to take over in a revolution that would be more or less inevitable. Once workers took over, everyone would share equally in the tools of production, choice of occupation would be free and fluid, and the ideal of liberated work would be realized.

His successors turned economics back into politics. They developed a theory of revolution, then built some of the twentieth century's greatest empires and most important movements around it, revising the theory as anomalous events kept cropping up and claiming the title "Marxist revolution." (Marx would never have expected revolution in proto-industrial Russia, much less preindustrial China.) It is difficult to overestimate the power that this idea has exercised. As long as variants of the revolutionary idea were in the mix, thinking about politics meant confronting certain questions. Are you for or against the radical transformation of society? Do you believe that Marx offered an irresistible portrait of human emancipation, or is the Marxist program just a new version of authoritarianism? And what are you going to do about it? However you answered, it had better be quickly and decisively, for the match was joined and in full swing. This was all the more true because for good parts of this century the contest has been not just between communism and some variety of democracy, but also between both of those and an explicitly authoritarian alternative willing to sacrifice liberty not to higher freedom but to political order and cultural and moral certainties. The challenge of fascism mattered as much as the promise of communism to many of the century's politically engaged figures, and more to some of the most serious of them.

The inescapable urgency of politics in recent times emerges in George Orwell's reflections on his own craft. In "Why I Write," that supremely political author described himself as "by nature" moved more by aesthetic pleasure, a journalist's instinct for reportage, and sheer egotism than by the desire to affect politics through writing. "In a peaceful age," he mused, "I might have written ornate or merely descriptive books, and might have remained almost unaware of my political loyalties." Instead, in direct response to his experience of the Spanish Civil War and the world war that it foreshadowed, "Every line of serious work that I have written since 1936 has been written, directly or indirectly, *against* totalitarianism and *for* democratic socialism, as I understand it. It seems to me nonsense, in a period like our own, to think that one can avoid writing of such subjects. Everyone writes of them in one guise or another."

Orwell's remarks illuminate why Thomas Mann, himself a student of the soul more than of the statehouse, could declare in the same period that "the

destiny of man presents itself in political terms."
Serious authors typically have something to say about
"the destiny of man," although they may not favor
so grand a phrase. This is all the more true in a
time when man's destiny is publicly up for dispute
and, more imposing, resolution. And, in Orwell and
Mann's time, hardly anyone could doubt that
politics—the movements of ideas, parties, classes, and
armies—was the field where this most serious cluster
of questions would be settled. There was no way out,
and looking for one meant not escape but escapism.

All of this seems esoteric, even alien, today. This is
a mark of how radically the scope of political aspiration has narrowed. In the early part of this century,
prominent intellectuals such as Edmund Wilson and
John Dewey took the idea of communism, and later
the idea of socialism, very seriously indeed. Their contemporary John Reed, one of the generation's most
gifted journalists, threw in his lot with the Soviet
cause, as did thousands of American writers, artists,
and ordinary citizens. No one could be a serious student of politics without coming to terms with the
same questions that exercised these figures. Senator
Joseph McCarthy may have been a paranoid and
ignorant man, but he was not mistaken in believing
that there were leftists who differed basically and
irreconcilably with him in positions of influence in
this country. The point of all this is not to revive those
debates—in important ways they are now too distant
to be revived—but to give some sense of how high and
how real the stakes of politics were then.

Those stakes did not depend on revolution alone. Setting aside that extreme idea, the fact is that until recently the nations of the world were motivated by several distinct kinds of political aspiration, and these shaped domestic politics everywhere. Some countries made Marx's ideal their official touchstone, often to horrific effect. Others, including Sweden and Germany, aimed at solidarity and economic fairness, creating systems that had as much in common with socialism as with the unrestrained market. Even more radical ambitions were in the mainstream of those countries' politics; there were unreconstructed Communists in the French government in the 1980s, and until 1990 the platform of the British Labour Party called for the nationalization of major industries. These competing visions made politics a choice among forms of society. Even in America, whose political spectrum has been less broad than most, the quasi-socialist Progressive Henry Wallace was a real presidential candidate in 1948 and Democrats as recent as George McGovern in 1972 advocated a politics with identifiable strains of European-style social democracy. Conservatives who talked about "creeping socialism" were not just engaging in demagoguery, but acknowledging that real questions about social and economic organization were in dispute in political decisions.

Even that margin of real disagreement seems gone today, and much of politics' power to stoke the imagination has gone with it. Politics around the world has drawn into a tight, neoliberal knot. Market policies

are in the ascendant from Stockholm through Delhi to
Jakarta, and the chief political questions revolve less
around fairness than in the orbit of efficiency. The
defining political event of the past decade has been
the economic, political, and moral failure of state
socialism, and the accompanying expansion of the
free market, with the collapse of the Soviet bloc providing the most dramatic instance. Even if it does not
prove the excellence of free markets, those countries'
legacy of poverty and repression provides a striking
case against the century's leading alternative to it. In
the same decade, the idea of a socialist path to development suffered what was probably its decisive defeat when India, home to 40 percent of the world's
poor after nearly fifty years of semi-socialist policies and often adamant socialist rhetoric, opened
itself to foreign investment and instituted market
reforms. Around the world, the International Mone-
tary Fund (IMF) has informed country after country
that international support comes attached to bud-
getary discipline and neoliberal market reforms.

Although there is grumbling about the prefabri-
cated character of IMF policy and other neoliberal
policies, which often make a Procrustean bed of
economists' beloved supply-and-demand curves, most
serious objections have been nearer quibbles than
denunciations. This is because the neoliberal ascent is
not construed as partisan thuggery but, at worst, as a
kind of mugging by history. Hardly anyone seriously
contemplates an alternative to the free market,
because no one has offered a plausible one. The social

democratic parties of Europe are left arguing around the edges of policy about how much of their countries' welfare nets to keep, and even the former Communists of Eastern Europe distinguish themselves from liberals on the *pace* of economic reform, not its appropriateness. Indeed, many old political distinctions have become almost meaningless in the face of economic demands. Poland's relatively successful transition to the free market was conducted by a government of former Communists, while the Czech Republic has foundered in corrupt privatization and unreformed medical and pension systems under Eastern Europe's most outspoken free-marketeer, Vaclav Klaus. India's nationalist Bhartiya Janata Party, which employed the rhetoric of economic self-reliance in its successful 1998 campaign, announced upon taking power that it would continue economic liberalization and that self-reliance was "a state of mind."

Of course, there are important questions about how best to make the new markets work. These, though, are very different from the questions of the past century. They ask, given existing institutions and political arrangements, "How shall we get there?" This is a technical question, however interesting and important. There is nothing here of the questions "Where shall we go? What shall we become?" which long made politics the site of the most basic moral question writ large.

Indeed, a great deal of this country's foreign policy is nowadays premised on the belief that we are all headed to the same place. American indulgence of

Chinese human-rights abuses finds its defense in the conviction that markets are ineluctable pacifiers, that governments that host McDonald's not only do not go to war with one another but eventually hold free elections and refrain from abusing their citizens. On this theory, economic liberty produces an independent middle class, which in turn forms a backbone of resistance against government abuses and, if only in defense of its own interests, will tend to push for free political institutions. According to this view, politics should stand back and let economics do its work. The empirical evidence for this idea is mixed, and countries from Brazil to China show that standing back can mean tolerating a parade of horrors. Because moral reactions recoil from such complacency, international human-rights advocacy attracts many committed women and men and has become one of the few growth areas in politics. However, it is an effort to nudge the rudder, often so slightly as only to save particular individuals, and is far from restoring the old idea that politics could remake the world.

The international collapse of world-making politics has coincided with the exhaustion—perhaps only temporary, but pervasive in the impression it has made—of a distinctly American strand of political transformation. Although American politics has seldom aimed to change the human predicament at large, its highest ambitions in this century have been to overcome two obdurate features of that predicament: racial division and poverty. To a certain extent in the New Deal period, and most dramatically in the

1960s, American politics was animated by the idea that these continuing crises could be put away for good by wise and magnanimous policies. The versions of welfare benefits, food stamps, and social medicine that came under congressional attack in 1996 were born in Lyndon Johnson's War on Poverty, a barrage of social programs whose aim was the end of widespread poverty in America.

One example is particularly telling. The recent touchstone issue in racial politics, affirmative action, was designed as a stopgap measure on the road to real equality of opportunity for black Americans, a road that supporters and skeptics of the policy alike believed the country had begun to follow. As Nathan Glazer observed in 1998 in *The New Republic*, no one who helped to design affirmative action believed that, thirty years later, it would be any kind of issue; it should have become superfluous and withered away.

Today, the significance of affirmative action in American culture has changed utterly. It is an emblem of the intractability of racial division, and of government's deep and ambiguous implication in those problems. For their defenders, the policies that were once tied to infinite optimism have become efforts at decency amid inequity that, although shrinking, shows no sign of disappearing. Affirmative action and that other legacy of the War on Poverty, welfare, are defended not because they promise to eliminate basic problems, but because ignoring those problems seems the more brutal as the problems come to seem ineliminable. Defenders of welfare policy today often find themselves saying, as opponents of the early policy might have, that the poor are always with us and cannot be wished or willed away. Politics may be our chief way of engaging these problems, but today it does not promise to overcome them.

It is important not to identify the American policies of the twentieth century with more radical, Promethean aims. The two are emphatically not the same. Human beings may not be able to make themselves other than they are, as the century's revolutionaries hoped; but they can surely better themselves, beginning from where they are, and that was the kernel of the American hope. The point, though, is that in these two related ambitions there has been a parallel narrowing. Americans who came of age after 1974 have never seen the government undertake a large-scale project other than highway maintenance and small wars, and relatively few are inspired by the idea that it should. Fewer still, even if they believe government ought to undertake such work, can say just how it should go about it. In this climate of modest skepticism and deep ambivalence, there is little sustenance for political hope.

All of this constrains any attempt to say what politics is for. Believing that politics can, in a phrase that can no longer be spoken without a reluctant irony, "change the world" provides a powerful response to this question. The political crusader was a prominent type in this country's politics for a very long time. Personified in public visionaries such as Martin Luther

King, Jr., it has fueled many politicians and many more activists who have devoted their lives to politics. Putting oneself on the right side of history, even hastening history's progress, is no mean project.

Moreover, both Promethean politics and the more modest American variant promise their participants something extraordinary: the achievement of their political aims, whether in their lifetimes or not, will redeem all their sacrifices. It will make their lives intelligible and worthwhile. To borrow a pair of religious terms, politics is eschatological in its promise to change human circumstance in elemental ways, and salvific in its power to give sense to our fragmented, frustrated, and suffering lives. So long as world-making politics is plausible, this attitude seems fitting, even noble. When such politics becomes implausible, the crusader's stance becomes quixotic in the original sense—an attempt to fill a role that no longer exists in the world. In the absence of a transformatory politics, whether we can find another way of of engaging our highest motives in politics has become a critical question.

The Therapeutic Reaction

Imagine a politics that makes everything better, that ends racial division, heals troubled neighborhoods, and replaces violence and smut with scenes of suburban pastoral serenity. Now imagine that this politics demands no effort, no conflict, and no sacrifice: to win these changes, we have only to say, very clearly and very sincerely, that we would like them, please. It sounds like something out of *The Wizard of Oz*, a ruby-slippered return to an idyllic Kansas.

It may also sound eerily familiar. This has been the tone of the decade's most visible effort to restore politics to its old power. It began in Hillary Clinton's much-derided, but really quite plaintive speech calling for a renewed "politics of meaning." That quasi-initiative dissipated into the ether of its own weightlessness: it was manifestly a sentiment rather than a proposal, something able to elicit a moment's sympathy but not so much as an afternoon's concrete work.

Still, the same idea has found some forms concrete enough to occupy ground of their own. They make up an inward turn of the Promethean spirit, replacing the aim of changing the world with a change in one's own emotions. For this reason, the type of politics that they inspire might be called "therapeutic politics." Although it is well-meaning, it does not find a way to turn intention into action. Indeed, it is a political version of the popular belief in the potency of fantasy.

The most ambitious exercise in therapeutic politics took the form of Bill Clinton's major "initiatives" in the year before scandal hamstringed his presidency. The kickoff was the president's community-service summit in Philadelphia. A bipartisan flock of politicians, advocates, and actual community members performed variations on the uncontroversial theme that community service is a good and needful thing. Clinton missed no chance to mention his Americorps program for young, full-time volunteers, and pounded a few nails. Then, having done their part for community service, the assembled went home. For people serving their communities every day, the summit brought nothing except a lingering confidence that both Clinton and 1996 Republican vice-presidential candidate Jack Kemp approve of their work.

The same air of ethereal goodwill has surrounded the administration's treatment of race, advertised as a centerpiece of Clinton's second term. The president notoriously proposed that white Americans issue an official apology to blacks for the nation's legacy of slavery and racial discrimination. He also suggested that, if an apology seemed too strong, we should at least undertake "a national discussion" about race. His own part in that "discussion" was occasional to the point of haphazardness. He appointed a "One America" panel, without any official power, charged with the task of "examining" race in America. The panel began by bickering over how white-Asian racism differs from white-black racism, was vexed by critics' observation that it included no opponents of affirmative action, and then dropped out of sight. It reemerged in September 1998 with no new policies or further initiatives, but with a proposal that it should be instituted permanently.

These examples are not aberrations. Their high profiles, moral impeccability, and vacuity make them exemplars of the therapeutic approach to politics. Many of the administration's headline-winning actions display the same spirit, albeit less starkly. In June 1997, Clinton convened a group of "business leaders, educators, and parent representatives" to talk about drawing up "voluntary standards" for sex and violence on the wild-west Internet. After front-page reports in *The Washington Post* and some weighty words about our common values, the effort disappeared. In August, Clinton garnered much attention by announcing a "$2.1 billion initiative" against diabetes that, on examination, amounted largely to pointing out long-established spending. That money is still being spent, as it was before the "initiative." This president has made a practice of catching the public's eye by doing very little with great moral gravity.

Politicians low on power or scruples have always preferred words to deeds. However, the current initiatives, summits, and crusades do not exude cynicism. Instead, they are most unsettling in their sincerity and the invitation they issue to take sincere speech as a substitute for action. More than a few observers have noted that President Clinton seems genuinely to believe whatever he happens to be saying at the moment—no matter its inconsistency with other declarations that he has equally believed in—and that he has an uncanny knack for drawing others into his transient conviction.

Yet there is something fruitless in these moments of shared sentiment. The idea of an apology does not address a ten-to-one disparity between white and black household wealth, or an equally unsettling disproportion between black men who go to prison and those who graduate from college. Sentiment in itself does not alter the social world. There is another problem as well, in the way that the president deployed the very idea of apology. An apology takes its force from reciprocity between a wrongdoer and a victim. If I apologize to you, I am acknowledging some particular harm that I have done, and at the same time recognizing your importance as a person: you matter, so harming you was wrong, and an apology is due. An apology undoes the suggestion that a knowing act of harm carries, that the person harmed is of inferior worth. This might fairly be called an act of moral restoration.

This reciprocity falters when we try to transplant it from personal relations to whole populations and institutions. When highly placed representatives of one population "apologize" to another entire population, the act is inescapably closer to posting a billboard than to extending a hand. An apology is most effective in addressing a discrete act where the hurt is chiefly in the act itself. The further the harm is embedded in a complex and continuing legacy of injustice, the less force an apology carries. "Apologizing" for the economic, social, and cultural circumstances that we now share amounts to lamenting those circumstances, not to doing anything about them. The injury that the apology ostensibly addresses now resides in those circumstances themselves. Apology cannot palliate that injury, for it is a daily reality.

A national apology for slavery, then, made no sense. As a meaningful act, it was not even possible. What is possible, though, is adopting the *rhetoric* of apology, with all its moral gravity, to lend the impression of gravity to a superficial declaration. The rhetoric describes something profound, and its skillful use is enough to create the illusion that something profound has happened, that things have been set right. The invocation of apology suggested that white Americans could enjoy the cleansing of conscience that actual apologies begin. It offered a way of feeling better without doing better. Talking in weighty, exhorting tones about community service has the same effect, and solemnly urging traditional values on multimedia marketers conveys a sense of moral accomplishment in the absence of fresh moral—or political—effort. This politics offers goodness, magnanimity, even absolution, all without work.

Politics' therapeutic turn has affinities with two trends. The first might be called Prozac morality, the idea that moral concern mainly involves the way a person feels about something. (I do not mean to deny that psychiatric drugs help many people to overcome emotional difficulties, often freeing them to deal with underlying problems. My point is that such drugs are easily misused in a culture that ignores root problems in favor of palliating symptoms.) The thing itself, racial inequality for example, is just the peg on which the person's emotions get hung. In this view, moral perception means not so much noticing that something is wrong as noticing that we feel bad about it. Moral action, then, means changing our feelings, and moral achievement means not altering the world, but reconciling ourselves to whatever we find there. If we can find a way to feel good about it, then it must be good.

It is hard not to see this attitude in the excesses of the psychiatric profession, where some irresponsible practitioners dispense pills to help people feel at home with any old thing. The same attitude is manifest in the suspicion among young professionals that it is gauche to say anything worse of a profession or life-style than that it is unfulfilling. Expressing a distaste for Wall Street because you don't want to work one-hundred-hour weeks with greedy, shallow colleagues is fine. Objecting that working on Wall Street amounts mostly to rearranging wealthy speculators' money smacks of self-righteousness, cant, and a failure to consider the feelings of one's peers who are beginning Wall Street jobs. Young brokers may acknowledge the social dubiousness of their work, and still feel good about it because they want the comforts of wealth; this is acceptable. However, anyone who insists that the work is simply inappropriate invites the favorite ironist technique, the reinterpretation of principles into psychological symptoms. What is making *him* so bothered? This view of personal morality more and more comes down to the idea that pleasant emotions are good, and that unpleasant emotions are in the end the only bad.

The short-lived call for apology echoed this attitude. Understanding that an apology would mainly benefit the consciences of the affluent, requesting an apology amounts to saying that the problem with racial inequity is that it disturbs some otherwise comfortable people. If this is true, then the solution is to find a way of making those people more comfortable. When they are sufficiently at ease, the problem will be gone. Whatever its merits as a matter of personal morality, this attitude is a sleeping draft for more traditional kinds of political engagement. It is no surprise, then, that this attitude has arisen when traditional political work is at its least credible.

Therapeutic politics also echoes the influence of identity politics. Identity politics, based on sex, sexuality, and, mostly, race and ethnicity, suggests that politics should work not so much to give people *things* such as education and jobs as to give them *recognition*. Identity politics asks, for instance, that white Americans acknowledge that black people matter, have worth and deserve respect, partly just because of who they are. In this view, the greatest political failures are failures of recognition, organized insults to particular groups.

This is not a silly or trivial idea. Recognition does matter. Sitting in the back of a bus in Alabama, for instance, is not a great inconvenience; when mandated by law, however, it declares that one group of citizens is inferior to another in the eyes of the state and the culture that it represents. A sodomy law, or the bans on miscegenation that lasted until the late 1960s in some states, need not be regularly enforced in order to announce that some couples are abnormal and beneath recognition. These are serious affronts.

However, identity politics harbors a peculiar susceptibility to misuse. Its concerns lend themselves to facile, rhetorical treatments in a way that more substantive political programs do not. Identity politics suggests that a major problem with the legacy of slavery is that it is caught up in a continuing disrespect of black Americans. There is surely truth in this. Now, if the president announces sincere regard and regret for blacks' experience of racism, allegedly on behalf of all white Americans, there is at least a fair pretext for saying that the demands of identity politics have been met. No one could make the same mistake about an apology's relevance to a politics that addressed itself to income inequality, the funding levels of inner-city schools, and the like.

Therapeutic politics presents risks beyond the political realm. Practices such as apology are essential to our lives. When these practices and the phrases that enact them are paraded as political devices, they are inevitably degraded. Faced with a public caricature of apology, we can hardly help suspecting that our private apologies somehow ape its aping. Any private expression of empathy, apology, or atonement must contend with the cheapening of those ideas in politics. If we make morality a hollow public ritual, we hollow out its private force as well. In this respect, therapeutic politics is connected to the proliferation of flattening irony.

Yet the greater risk is not private but public. Moral rhetoric without action produces a gradual separation of politics from reality. Politicians' rhetoric has always flirted with fantasy, but at the same time politics depends on the conviction that, sometimes, saying is a way to doing. Where all connection between saying and doing fails, politics dies.

We have a powerful reminder of this truth today in the new democracies of Eastern Europe. From Czech president Vaclav Havel to politically active young Hungarians who spoke with me when I visited Budapest in 1992, the dissidents who overthrew that region's authoritarian regimes describe growing up in two worlds: the official reality of politicians' declarations and the actual experience of everyday life under authoritarian institutions. In their moving recollections, attaining democracy meant connecting word and deed in truth. We do not have to contemplate authoritarianism to recognize what is lost when political speech no longer touches the reality that most people inhabit. With this disconnection, politics becomes empty of everything except its own sterile self-certainty. Therapeutic hopes push our politics toward this cheery vacuum.

Whatever its virtues, politics is far from being an efficient way of making people feel better about themselves. Just as Hollywood will ordinarily outdo Washington for entertainment value, so real therapy or real drugs will attract many more self-seekers than the politics of Prozac morality. It is instructive to note that the enthusiasts of therapeutic politics have mainly been politicians and other public figures, people committed to—or caught in—public institutions and trying to find a way out of the ambivalence and cynicism that afflict those places now. This is not a way of winning converts but an attempt to rally the wavering faithful. Therapeutic politics is politics' capitulation to a culture withdrawn from politics.

Restoring the Public?

It is the paradox of politics that it tries to render itself unnecessary. With few exceptions, credible answers to the question "What is politics for?" do not lie in politics itself. Instead, the aim of politics is to secure ways of life outside the political realm. The Constitution's political structure protects private lives and voluntary associations, and that is for most people its defining accomplishment. The nineteenth-century American abolitionists joined a public battle to enable blacks to lead decent, private lives, as persons rather than property; politics was for them a necessary means, but not at all an end. For the architects of the War on Poverty, success would have meant the near-disappearance of poverty programs, just as civil rights leaders and their allies thought of affirmative action as a temporary measure that would disappear with the coming of a fair economy. By and large, we want not to be Congresspersons or crusaders, but to have our lives. Politics is the way to secure and better those lives.

Even the most extreme Promethean ambitions embrace this paradox. Marx believed that the coming of communism would mark the end of politics. In revolution, politics would liquidate itself, never to be revived. Politics was only a way to freedom. Hence, it is little surprise that the contemporary attitudes that most celebrate individual self-creation, whether in the hyperbole of *Wired* or the more measured tones of *Fast Company*, range from passing indifference to downright hostility toward politics. According to these attitudes, individual liberation has been achieved, or is just beyond the next horizon. The freedom of the Digerati or the Free Agent includes freedom from politics. Through the lens of this conviction, politics looks like a needless obsession with the unexciting affairs of unfree people.

Keeping in mind that politics does not exist for its own sake helps to make clear why some of the political forms of the past century look so strikingly like deformations. The Promethean aim required a devotion to politics that, if the revolution were not coming soon, would become a joyless ritual observance. Oscar Wilde once observed, "The trouble with socialism is that it takes too many evenings." If socialism is all evening meetings from now to eternity, with no better world ahead, then it is a joyless doctrine indeed. At the opposite end of the spectrum of political commitment, the contemporary perception of politics as a self-contained, parochial game is especially bleak, because politics that lacks purposes outside itself has no purpose at all. The contemporary politician comes close to resembling Wilde's eternal socialist, plus some money and influence, but minus even the expectation of a world improved by his efforts.

What, then, are the prospects of politics? At what does it appropriately aim, and which of its aims are

still viable? Each of the attitudes that I have been sur-
veying gives its own assessment of these questions.
For the Promethean attitude, politics is a fulcrum on
which we can turn the great themes of human existence and change our situation so basically that it
might be said that we become a different sort of being;
had Rousseau's or Marx's vision succeeded, politics
would have penetrated and reworked both the grand-
est arenas of history and the most intimate spaces of
personal experience. The therapeutic attitude aims at
equally dramatic change, but its starting point is different: rather than invade history to reshape the
human soul, it enters the soul in order to give history
a new direction. The ambition is the same, but the
path is reversed.

The third attitude is the despairing, skeptical one,
insisting that politics withdraw from these farther
fields. Politics here is a narrow matter of the institutions of governance—not so much their wise use as
jockeying for control over them. Anything more
ambitious is overreach and confusion: anachronistic
and possibly dangerous when it aims at transformation, mainly nostalgic and fatuous in the therapeutic
program. Politics here is writ small and kept small,
able to do little harm and mainly unrelated to our real
moral ambitions.

This is not an inviting set of choices. If we were
free to decide between selecting one of them and judg-
ing against politics altogether, we might well take the
second course. Many people today believe they have
done exactly that. This belief demands the question

whether we are at liberty to make that choice at all. I find that I cannot reflect on this question without thinking of a figure who must, at first, seem remote to a discussion of contemporary American politics and culture: the sixteenth-century Frenchman Michel de Montaigne. The first reason that Montaigne belongs here, his age and nationality notwithstanding, is that he is in a real sense the father of the modern form of ironic skepticism. There is an unknowing echo of him in Seinfeld and in the view of politics as cynical game-playing.

Montaigne comes down to us as an essayist, the inventor of the essay in its modern form and, perhaps more important, the modern father of writing as a form of self-exploration. Rousseau saw in him the beginning of "studying the human heart by reading the lives of individuals," the method shared by two groups—novelists and psychologists—whose work does much to define modern experience. His reflections on the squalid backstage of human motivation, and on the failure of pious declaration to indicate good character or produce sound action, led him to issue what could be a motto for contemporary ironists: "There are two things that I have always observed to be in accord: supercelestial thought and subterranean conduct." Montaigne would have appreciated, and could no doubt have topped, the cynic's declaration of a later century: "The more he spoke of his honor, the faster we counted our spoons."

Unlike many contemporary skeptics, however,

Montaigne drew his ironic attitude from long experience of the worst in human nature. He wrote in the time of the European wars of religion, following the Protestant Reformation, when the battle between the old faith and the new literally divided nations, cities, and families, including Montaigne's own. The atrocities of the war were horrible, and to a Catholic of Montaigne's disposition, a believer who considered human reason unable to answer ultimate questions, they were also futile. The questions that were advertised to underlie the wars were inaccessible to any answer other than faith. Montaigne, like today's ironist, saw politics as a symptom, a too-often violent expression of the urges of pride, ambition, and self-righteousness, wearing the trappings of conviction.

Although he thought that his was a disastrous time, Montaigne suspected that most of human history, especially on the stage of politics, was a litany of disaster. He was educated in the classics in a way that is unthinkable today, speaking nothing but Latin until the age of seven, and was in his own mind nearly a contemporary of the ancient authors he admired. He filled his essays with accounts of the bloodshed, pointless and misdirected warfare, and willful cruelty of every age that had preceded his. He pondered the violence of Aztec sacrifices as a perverse doppelganger of the atrocities that Europeans inflicted on the New World, and on one another in their own wars. Wherever others might find a window of hope, he saw a dark mirror.

For all that, when Montaigne withdrew to his

study to begin the *Essays*, he had already served several terms as mayor of Bordeaux and made a small career as a royal adviser and negotiator in the wars of religion. Moreover, his years of writing produced an extraordinary result. Rather than repudiate public affairs in favor of private pleasures and small, intimate perfections, Montaigne devoted many of his pages to exploring the unhappy circumstances that he shared with his countrymen and his ancient contemporaries as a common problem in which everyone was bound up and with which any honest man had to contend. He shaped the *Essays* in the hope that illuminating cruelty and dangerous self-certainty would be a way to overcoming them.

His characteristic essay is an unsettling assault on certainty, in which he sets off one view against another, moving among them with a bewildering capacity to make one seem as plausible as the last yet no more so than the next. The upshot of these displays is a lingering, slightly accusatory question: Why should you think you are right? Are you not just being arrogant and prideful? And what harm might your self-certainty lead you to do? He strengthened the accusation with grim, sometimes wrenching evocations of massacres, torture, and wrongful execution performed by men too confident to doubt themselves.

At the same time, Montaigne developed a picture of how a person might participate in politics without surrendering to its evils. Above all, he urged a constant wariness against one's own capacity for excessive conviction. "It is right," he wrote, "that things

should touch us, providing they do not possess us."
He was, he said, "attached to the general and just
cause only with moderation and without feverish-
ness," without "penetrating and mortgaging commitments" that would compromise his own judgment
and conscience. To permit political commitments to
become "penetrating" would be akin to forging one's
soul as a weapon of politics: "We have no need to
harden our hearts with those plates of steel. It is
enough to harden our shoulders. It is enough to dip
our pens into ink, without dipping them into blood."
He would never permit himself to become morally
identical with any party or program, and insisted that
he was more skeptical of his allies and admiring of his
enemies than the reverse. He saw no other way to join
in politics without drowning in it.

But why join in it at all? That Montaigne decided
in favor of politics, not particularly as a good thing,
but as necessary and so morally inescapable, is perhaps the most impressive quality of his work. His reason was that the unhappy blend of base motivation,
high thought and rhetoric, and terrible action that he
feared and despised was a universal problem. He
wrote, "There never was any opinion so disordered as
to excuse treachery, disloyalty, tyranny, and cruelty,
which are our ordinary vices." These terrible "vices"
were both inexcusable and "ordinary," widespread
and everyday. They could not be eliminated, and perceiving them acutely created certain responsibilities.
One of these was the obligation to combat them in the
public world, not least by serving quietly and resisting

their urges. To imagine that, just because the ordinary vices moved powerfully through politics, they could be overcome by abandoning politics was a self-serving delusion.

So, as one who loved peace, good company, and the spirit of tolerance, Montaigne was obliged to call pride and cruelty by their right names, to bring them to light, and to use public means to keep alive the possibility of a civilized society. Out of horror he developed a sense of irony; but out of irony he formed an impassioned ambivalence toward politics. He practiced and urged a politics that did not aim to change the world, but might help to keep alive some of its best possibilities.

This is an idea that politics forms a necessary portion of an interminable grappling with evils that may prove ineliminable, devoted to the preservation of imperfect but invaluable goods. In Montaigne's tradition followed a strand of thinkers who do not consider the human condition through the lens of politics, but instead make their way to politics through the human condition. Montaigne's countryman Albert Camus was among these, as, arguably, was George Orwell, although both were deeply colored by the aims of times very different from Montaigne's. Perhaps the finest American member of this tradition is Thoreau, whose *Walden* remains, despite superficial popular characterizations, an extraordinary document of reflection on the extent and nature of personal responsibility for common things.

Could we reach the same conclusions about our

politics that Montaigne did about his, that it is necessary, and for reasons that are not, mainly, regrettable? We might doubt the possibility. After all, he and most of his descendants wrote against the backdrop of terrible political dramas, while we observe above all the banality of our public life. Still, we may have available to us a way of thinking about politics that displays some of Montaigne's spirit. Perhaps it is better to say that this is a way of thinking about public life. It begins in the recognition that, contrary to the fantasy of the moment, public life and public institutions can never be obsolete. Our private lives—our work, our families, our circles of friends—are pervasively affected by things that can never be private: law and political institutions, economics and culture. We ignore these essentially public matters at the risk of misunderstanding our own well-being. And that misunderstanding invites us to neglect public concerns in ways that impoverish the public realm and, in time, erode the underpinnings of good private lives. Indeed, the interdependence of public and private is so great that speaking of them as separate is often misleading.

We might conclude that public life continues to matter, not because it changes us fundamentally, but because it is our only way of contending with tasks that we may never complete but cannot permit ourselves to neglect. These are tasks of maintenance, keeping intact both private life and the public life that is caught up with it. They do not preclude transformation of certain kinds; rather, they precede and preserve it. Sometimes maintenance requires cultivating our best qualities, sometimes it means recognizing and resisting our worst, and it always requires keen attention to where we are, what we are becoming, and what we think it fitting for us to be. It is what the prevailing approaches to politics have failed to be—a way of understanding what we do in public work, and why that work is necessary and good.

CHAPTER THREE

The Practice of the Public

Each one of them, withdrawn into himself, is almost unaware of the fate of the rest. Mankind, for him, consists in his children and his personal friends. As for the rest of his fellow citizens, they are near enough, but he does not notice them. He touches them but feels nothing.

—*Alexis de Tocqueville,* Democracy in America

SOMETIMES words get away from us. They come unmoored from the things they represent. Nearly everyone has repeated a common word dozens of times until it suddenly becomes unfamiliar, a collection of foreign sounds divorced from their familiar meaning. This can bring a feeling like vertigo, a dizzy uncertainty that anything is as it seems.

The easier way to lose a word, though, is to stop thinking about it. When we use a word long enough in conventional fashion, we can lose all track of its meaning. We can lose sight of the fact that it has stopped having meaning. Some words come to be like ghosts, roaming among us without flesh, vaguely recalling old dramas and tragedies that the living have forgotten.

One of our leading phantoms is the word *public*. Like many ghosts, it has a distinguished—but in this case not a royal—heritage. It comes from the Latin *publius*, the people. It is the source of *republic*, the realm ruled by the people; its homeliest cousin is the beer-serving *pub*, a shortened version of *public house*. During the fierce debates of the 1780s over what form the American constitution should take, James Madison and other revolutionary leaders wrote their pamphlets under the pseudonym Publius. The idea of speaking for the public was important enough in the young republic that the most serious and high-minded figures tried to personify the *publius;* where the public rules in principle, its personification rules in fact.

Now, the word has lost its realm. Its uses are like the scattered provinces of a broken empire. We speak of *public* not in itself, but just as part of other phrases, which we use mainly without thought. We have public schools, attend to (or scoff at) public opinion, hear about but do not attend public meetings, and doubt the existence of public servants and public intellectuals. Of these, perhaps the most revealing is the set of connotations that comes with the *public* in public school—and public parks, public rest rooms, and public clinics. These are the second-rate versions of their private counterparts. They are run-down. If they are indoors, they smell of disinfectant spread over a layer of grime. The people who use them are the poor, the unlucky, and the unambitious.

So in its most widespread version, the public is what the government provides to those who cannot get a share of the private. The libertarian Charles Murray expresses a pervasive perception when he writes, "The reality of daily life is that, by and large, the things the government does tend to be ugly, rude, slovenly—and not to work. Things that private organizations do tend to be attractive, courteous, tidy—and to work. That is the way America really is."

Then there is "public opinion," the opinion ascribed by pollsters and pundits to "the American people." By and large, this has become shorthand for uninformed attitudes dignified by statistical aggregation. Public opinion is gathered by simpleminded phrasings of complex questions, demanding yes-and-no answers, that might have been designed to make their respondents appear foolish. It is not to be taken seriously, to be weighed in any one person's own deliberations—except, those of a politician plotting tactics.

After all, we take an opinion seriously because we respect the character and judgment of the woman or man who holds it, or because we are convinced by the reasons behind it. Neither of these gives us reason to hold public opinion in high regard. It comes to us anonymously, without arguments, and with the statistical near-certainty that some contribution to it comes from individuals for whom we would have no particular esteem were we to encounter them in person. Just as public facilities are a shoddy version of private ones, public opinion is a crude jumbling-together of private attitudes, a composite of snapshots taken in unposed and sometimes untoward circumstances.

Then there are phrases that seem outmoded, especially *public servant* and *public intellectual*. They both suggest that there is a special ethical quality in the idea of the public. A public servant works for the public; but the point is not where she draws her paycheck, not who employs her, but what she serves. A public servant, in the quaint phrase, serves some idea of the public good. With our dim view of politics, it is unsurprising that we would be as likely to speak of a public servant as of a water closet. *Politician* or *bureaucrat* will suffice for us. Neither of those words carries the intimations of ethical expectation that perch anachronistically on *public servant* like a top hat or hoop skirt on a contemporary mannequin.

Public intellectual is similarly vexed. A public intellectual concerns herself with matters that are, somehow, specifically public. We do have figures like this, but they are more and more overshadowed by celebrity intellectuals, notable less for the seriousness of their ideas than for their novelty and brass. They shock and titillate, or they intrigue by offering new explanations for our discontents, our neuroses, our disappointing bodies. They increasingly play the same role as the advocates of faddish diets, or the performer of the season's hit song. They satisfy the desire that something should be going on to draw one's attention, provide some stimulation, give a feeling of ferment. Then, by and large, they are gone.

Public Deprivation

The usual antonym of *public*, *private*, is a curious word. Etymologically, it refers to the lack of something, to deprivation. Historically it meant being without the dignity of public authority, status, and recognition. The private man was a man deprived.

Now, we invest *private* with all the dignity that it once lacked. In a way, it has changed places with *public*. Rather than deprivation, privacy bespeaks possession and achievement. What is private is our own, and we are known by it. Private schools and hospitals are the best, designed to attend to our needs as we suspect public institutions will not. Their excellence is an acknowledgment of the quality of their patrons. Private clubs, beaches, and even communities are the mark of prestige, the signature of social and economic arrival. The status and personal authority that once belonged to public position are now creatures of private achievement instead. Even many of our monuments are private creations, from the mansion of Bill Gates near Seattle to the new Getty Museum in Los Angeles.

The private realm commands our attention and respect. It is the site of accomplishment, and of accomplishment's display. However, its priority does not end there. Private life is also the almost exclusive home of our highest satisfactions. As *Fast Company* understands, careers are at the center of many lives today. Our work is how we think of ourselves, and how we are known. It occupies not only time, but also emotional and intellectual energy. It is the source of our perceptions of dignity and personal worth, our position in the world, the résumé that enables us to meet new people and move with confidence among familiar ones. An occupation is our way of securing and announcing who we are in a time when proving oneself is a never-finished task. In colonial and revolutionary America, New England's villages chose selectmen, public officials whose status made them something like elders of the civic church. Today, the ranks of status are filled by self-selection, and careers are the chief way that we jockey for place.

Beside the private life of careers is the private world of family and affection. Here as well we cultivate some of our greatest pleasures. If our time is devoted to professional achievement, it is also intensely concerned with the cultivation of personal excellence. Psychological well-being, physical health, and various forms of spiritual ambition employ vast swathes of the publishing industry and an entire sector of trainers and consultants. We want to be not only successful, but also good, in mind and body alike. In this respect, the therapeutic entrepreneur of *Fast Company* is much nearer the spirit of the age than the classic self-sacrificing striver. Our varieties of self-improvement are intensely personal. They aim to enhance the personal realm by making its relationships more open and caring, its recreation more demanding and pleasurable, and its duration longer by perhaps a decade of life. We have high hopes for ourselves and the people we love, and they are mainly private hopes.

However, there is still a residue of the old idea of deprivation in our celebration of private things. Our emphasis on the private is a concession that many of the good things we cultivate alone are unavailable elsewhere. Private life is so much a reprieve, an emotional and erotic haven or temple of self-improvement, partly because many of us feel the need to retreat from other reaches of our lives. Despite the currency of *Fast Company*'s ideal, it is difficult to see much of the work we do as something we would want to bring home, that would enrich our most intimate connections if the two realms were woven together. It is even less plausible that public matters, like our degraded and disappointing politics, could make our private lives better. Admitting these into our homes would only color the intimate realm in the grays, or the garishness, of those alternatingly bleak and absurd arenas. Private life becomes the sole place where we can exercise the trust and care, the sense of good purpose, that seem to have little safe purchase elsewhere.

Our commitment to private careers, also, has something to do with a fear of having to rely on public institutions that may serve us badly. I have had more than a few conversations, on evening-shaded West Virginia porches and over crowded Harvard dining tables, with people who believe that a responsible adult must at least provide her family with private education, private medical care, and a house in a

prosperous neighborhood. These people are not especially greedy, nor are they driven social climbers. They
take seriously an idea of responsibility. They are sure
that they cannot rely on anything but their own purchasing power to educate their children, keep their
families healthy, and provide a modicum of the space,
clean air, and sunlight that form the landscape archi-
tecture of national identity.

All of these concerns, however pressing they seem,
yield pride of place to the pervasive worry about
securing a retirement. It is difficult to convey to a
member of an older generation how convinced young
people are that no public institution can be relied on
to provide for them, no matter the contributions they
are now required to make to it. The anticipated collapse of Social Security may have more practical, psychological effect on the current generation than the
atomic bomb had on its predecessor. The presumption
that Social Security will not last another generation is
as widespread as it is ill-understood; it is less a judgment of fact than a declaration of pessimistic mood. It
rests not on careful economic analysis, but on an
accurate perception of the popular temper.

The note of deprivation in all of this is hard to
miss. The sense that public space has fallen into irremediable neglect draws young people into a private
space where they see their best opportunity for a
decent life. Although it is an affirmation of that private life, their choice is also both constrained and con-
straining. They choose as they do in part because the
prospect of relying on failing public institutions is

almost coercively grim. Out of wariness as much as out of love, they take safe paths early, and mainly cleave to them. They sense that there is a loss here, but that no better way is open to them.

The atrophy of public things and the celebration of private life form an elaborate exercise of isolation and neglect. We can isolate private life from the larger world by abandoning care for whatever is not private. We can also isolate it by leaving behind the devotions and strictures of private life, the rules of decency that govern our intimate relations, when we enter the demanding world of work or, occasionally, politics. The question this separation requires is whether we can afford the neglect that we allow ourselves. We are engaged in a gamble that turning away from public things will not jeopardize our private goods, that we are neither morally obliged nor practically beholden to common things. Whether that gamble is well founded is, accordingly, an urgent question.

A Fitting Dependence

The troubled condition of those old ideas, the public and the private, is bound up with our skilled practice of neglect. By one means or another, we find ways of believing that the world does not need us, and that we do not much need it. For the ironist, this is almost entirely a matter of evasion. An attenuated species of autonomy accompanies the reluctance to develop any but superficial connections and reliances. This is not exactly a declaration of independence, not the bold pronouncement of "Invictus"—"I am the master of my fate, I am the captain of my soul"—instead, it is a studied refusal of obligation, a cultivated insubstantiality of devotion. The ironist keeps his own mind and heart private, and they are not enriched by their isolation.

When we are not ironic but credulous, when we watch the skies for angels, we engage in another kind of neglect. We refuse to attend to the obdurate, and often disappointing and restrictive, reality around us. We permit ourselves a bouquet of hopes and pleasures, but not ones that can ever come into contact with the rough surfaces and uneven heft of actual things. This is a species of willful confusion, imagining that the world shares the shape of our private idyll. In politics, this is the attitude of the therapeutic exhorter. Against the ironist's overtaxed suspicion, it presents an untested self-satisfaction and satisfaction with the state of things.

The most elaborate method of neglect belongs to the Free Agent and the Digerati. They see clearly the real world that the ironist evades and the angel watcher overlooks, and they are determined to escape it. In the eyes of the Free Agent, most lives, jobs, and communities are regrettable affairs, tangled heaps of happenstance that have hardened into routine and necessity. Constraint is everywhere, and it imposes a life that is undignified, banal, graceless. In response, these figures propose that personal grace, satisfying community, and good work are possible only for those who have left behind ordinary things in favor of what is utterly new, original, and idiosyncratic. The good life is one that is utterly one's own, lived apart from smaller existences.

All of these methods of neglect are tests of an idea that has a history. This is the idea that, in the words of John Milton's Satan, "the mind is its own place, and can make a hell of heaven, a heaven of hell." This is the aim of the ironist's psychic and emotional independence. If possible, it is even more the spirit of those who literally make their heaven by introducing divine hosts into the sublunary realm. We are engaged in a test of the power of the individual mind to make a world apart from the one in which it is actually set.

With the Free Agent and the Digerati, the idea becomes more radical. Milton's phrase breaks the individual free from the world, granting each person her own perceptions, desires, and loyalties, no matter how impudent or perverse they may seem to others. In the higher Prometheanism of our contemporaries, the mind's freedom is not complete until it can turn back on the world, reworking it, literally making "a heaven of hell." The *Wired* hero does not simply insist on the autonomy of his wishes, but indulges them through virtual reality or electronic self-enhancement, redeeming the promise that "you can be anything you want to be." The Free Agent is the thoroughgoing architect of his own life. For these figures, the mind is its own place, and the world is its place also.

These are the ideas that we are now testing against experience. They are unlikely to stand the test. What we should expect to find is that independence is not the essential quality of a mind or personality. On the contrary, we are in every respect testaments to our own thoroughgoing dependence. Thought that we recognize as wise or witty, behavior that is gracious or elegant, desire refined beyond mere hunger and rut, is all a portion of an inheritance. No one invents such everyday excellences; we all take them up and make them our own by acting in a way that confirms we have understood them.

The exercise of a good mind, or a good personality, is the accomplishment not of escaping a tradition of thought, speech, and behavior but of having understood its elements well enough to make them one's own reflectively, to sort and distinguish among them. This freedom displays itself in a kind of propriety, or fittingness, that is twofold. A person's ideas and manner sit naturally together, and fit her disposition as well. At the same time, she is able to respond—to other people, to ideas, to familiar or unfamiliar circumstances—in a way that is appropriate both to her and to the situation. She knows what she is about, in the several senses that this fruitfully ambiguous phrase allows. She knows what matters to her, what her purposes are; she knows what she is doing, what she is up to; and she knows what is around her, that is, she knows her setting. In all of this lies the dignity of familiarity with oneself, one's work, and one's place.

This kind of intelligence is no small achievement, and no one achieves it alone. The fortunate among us take a great deal of it from our parents and immediate families, not always (or even usually) from their avowed principles, but from the patterns that their consistent tone and repeated acts present. They show us what is ordinary, what we can expect from the world and from ourselves.

When a neglectful local government lets public schools languish, do you shrug in resignation or run for the local school board and, enduring vilification and harassing phone calls, spend six years working in small ways and large to improve education in your community? My mother did the second, and whatever sense I have of political responsibility I owe to that example. Her actions amounted to a steady insistence, never translated into as many words, that making laws and public institutions effective and humane is one of the charges we receive when we settle in any place. It was often not pleasant work; instead it was a reminder that to imagine that all our work should be pleasant is childish.

When a day's work comes to no good, or the project you have been slowly and scrupulously assembling collapses in your hands, are you angered by the unfairness of things or do you acknowledge the misfortune and think how much worse it would be to let your spirits be ruined by resentment? My father, somehow, always seems to feel the second. His is not the good luck of a thoughtlessly happy temper, but a steadiness suggesting that he has thought about the value of resentment and judged it worthless. Watching him, I think I have learned some of this. Watching further, I think I see that he learned it from his father.

These inheritances do not come only from our families. I had the happy fortune to grow up in a community where adults and young people could be friends. Many of my friends were singular: a charismatic born poet, a construction worker by trade and motorcyclist by vocation, who showed me that words and images can be made to dance and offered as shimmering tokens of affection; a Manhattan-trained ballerina who settled in West Virginia to teach dance and art to rural children, whose frank and sincere idealism has entered my thought as a bright, sharp blade against the easy grain of cynicism; a couple, educated at Yale, she now a small-town lawyer and he, among myriad community projects, a farmer and amateur blacksmith, who lectured me on radical economic theory and American labor history as we put up loose hay with his horses, and elicited from me a delight in ideas that has never left me. The memory of each of them, as one picture of how a person can live, forms a stay against the mind's impulse to collapse into the conventions of each new place, and to surrender to the disappointments of each moment.

These may be banal examples, but precisely this kind of invaluable banality sustains our human world. Ignoring it in favor of the romance of personal Prometheanism means neglecting the ground of our humanity. It means forgetting the encounters and experiences that enable us to remember what we might wish to be, and why.

This, I suspect, is why the ironic temperament becomes exhausted so easily. It begins from the idea that each of us should be radically independent, should generate ourselves from our own will and imagination. When that ambition disappoints, and his phrases and acts do not glisten with newness, the ironist treats his own derivative behavior with the vague contempt that a selfishly expectant parent might show toward a child who fails to perform. Refusing to take seriously such mundane things as the familiar vocabularies of thought, friendship, and romance, he stops his knowledge of them at a pointedly superficial conversance. And superficial conversance is not enough for intelligence, not enough to form a personality. *Mundane* comes from the Latin *mundus*, "the world"; by avoiding mundanities, we avoid the world, and by that avoidance we risk ignorance of what is good in it—and what is not.

Naturally, our local webs of dependence on family and friends are only the beginning. These implicate us in broader schemes of mutual reliance—not always directly but not only notionally either. For it is not too much to say that there is no good, or beautiful, or healthy thing in the world that does not depend for its origin and continued existence on the well-being of a host of other such things. The families in which we may be fortunate enough to learn can by and large exist only in intact communities, places where it is possible to live and work in peace and with some measure of dignity. Those communities persist only in regions and nations of relative peace and security. History provides enough instances of what can happen when these webs are torn. Today's examples are the crime and alcoholism of the former Soviet Union; the brutality of conscripted child soldiers in the wars of central Africa, where colonialism, Cold War proxy battles, and domestic power struggles have left regions and sometimes nations in lawless battles of all against all; and the savagery of the Balkans.

In all of this there lurks an idea of responsibility. In valuing any good thing, we also, if we are consistent, value the many good things on which it relies. If we value something in honesty, we recognize a certain responsibility for it beyond our pleasure in its momentary availability. Just by living in the world, just by caring for things, we take on a responsibility for the world's well-being. This is not meant to be that elusive philosophers' goal, the irresistible argument for moral behavior. I mean simply that the ironic reluctance to rest much hope on people, relationships, or institutions may be founded on a mistaken idea: that it is possible to *decide* whether or not to place such hope. In fact, so far as we care for anything at all, we must hope for a great deal from a great number of people, institutions, and relationships in which whatever we immediately care for is caught up. So the question is not whether to hope, but whether to acknowledge our hope, to make it our own. And hope and responsibility are the same here. In both, we tie our success or failure to the state of something outside us, which we cannot entirely control. We can refuse responsibility, but we cannot decide against its existence.

Commonplace Responsibility

Just over a year after graduating from Harvard, I met a former classmate at a birthday party in New York City. He is a warm young man, sincerely affectionate toward other people and sincerely hopeful that they should like him. He was eager to tell me about his first year as a college graduate. He had been working as an investment banker, and his work had taken him to West Virginia, a visit not many of my fellow students had made. We spent a few minutes tracing his travels, and concluded that he had passed within ten miles of my home. I asked whether he remembered the shape of the hills there, an irregular, ragged gentleness that I have seen nowhere else. Anyone who has not seen or does not recall them has difficulty imagining their lines, and I thought from his response that he remembered.

Then I asked what he had been doing in my hills. His response began with the sort of chuckle that announces a partial disowning of whatever is to follow it. He had been brokering deals among coal companies, making arrangements for mountaintop-removal strip-mining projects. I had spent a part of that spring in the coalfields, so his technical phrase had vivid reality for me. Mountaintop removal involves tearing apart the upper reaches of a mountain with dynamite, stripping away the layers of coal that run between levels of rock, and bulldozing the resulting rubble into the surrounding valleys. Sometimes mining companies remove as many as five hundred vertical feet from a mountain; more often, they dynamite to a depth of two or three hundred feet. Generally, the buried valleys and the ruined mountains meet midway, creating stretches of broken plateau. The hardwood forests that cover the region do not return to these fields of clay, shale, and stone, where only tough grasses and scrub trees grow. The violence of mountaintop removal has effectively closed down communities with the bad luck to sit at the feet of strip-mined mountains.

I do not remember whether I asked, "Why do you do it?" It is possible that, with that initial chuckle, he had acknowledged that we would be getting around to the question anyway. Either way, his answer was something extraordinary. It was all, he explained, the inevitable logic of the global market. People need energy, and they want it cheap. Coal companies can provide it more cheaply than anyone else. The coal executives who make the decisions that remove mountaintops would lose their jobs if they declined to make those choices. They would be replaced by other people, who would make exactly the decisions their predecessors had refused. If the highest officers did not opt for mountaintop removal, their companies would go bankrupt, and other mining outfits would strip the mountains they had saved. Investment bankers like him were in the same position.

There was more. The world economy was pulling apart between rich and poor, he told me. The warnings that American wages would be "leveled downward" as First World and Third World workers increasingly competed for the same jobs were probably true. The world's poorest countries would gain something in the process, but the real winners would be people like him, members of the financial elite who could help newly mobile capital on its way. The course of things was set. While he couldn't say that he endorsed it, he saw no reason to be on the losing side.

I do not mean to say whether he is right about the course of history or the nature of markets. His terms were polemical, adamant but imprecise. "The global market" and "capitalism" rarely help one to get one's bearings in a serious conversation. Still, there was something representative in his attitude. A sense that the drift of things is inevitable has set in among many young people. The idea that the direction of history, however hell-bent, will not change is a virtual license to ignore doubts about a practice such as mountain-top removal. Not every young investment banker in pursuit of his first ten million has thought things through in just these terms. For many, the Free Agent's creed is enough; for some, although fewer than some would imagine, greed is sufficient; but many grant that acquiescence is near the core of their work, and offer in defense only the thought that acquiescence may be the appropriate response to the present moment. They are not so much ushering in the next millennium as riding out the last.

There is a crude way of understanding the relationship between indifference to politics and the personal Prometheanism of *Fast Company* and my less giddy classmate. Although crude, it seems to me to be essentially right. It can be captured in a despairing formula: "You can't change the world, so you might as well get ahead in it."

If what I have been proposing is correct, then there are two mistakes in this formula. The first is the idea that "changing the world" is the standard for political work. This is the legacy of Promethean politics, whose failures are now obvious and whose ambitions no longer attract young people seeking purpose. In this respect, my investment banker was as Marxist in his idea of political change as in his analysis of economics. However, this proposal ignores the possibility that there might be a way of thinking about politics, or public life, that does not rely on the aim of transformation. It ignores the idea of a politics that begins in acceptance of our myriad, intrinsic responsibilities. This would be a politics not so much of transformation as of maintenance, of tending to human possibilities more than radically reworking them.

The second mistake is the conclusion "You might as well get ahead." If politics cannot change the world, then the choice between assuming and ignoring public responsibility is indifferent. Once transformation is out of the question, the vague realm of "public concern" is thought to be something that will take care of itself. But if everything we care for links us to a thousand other sources of well-being, then we emphatically had not "as well" be indifferent to those. The choice remains a choice, but we should not imagine that nothing is at stake in it beyond our own satisfaction. That is a dangerous misunderstanding.

The inheritance of Promethean politics, then, is complicit in a confused idea of our alternatives, one that winds up favoring personal Prometheanism. Thinking more clearly about these questions may help us to recover a more modest, but also more compelling picture of politics, or public life, and of our proper relation to it. I draw the distinction because by "public life" I mean something more than is usually intended by "politics." This view of public life might be captured by the image of "the commons," traditionally an unfenced region of a pastoral community, where everyone is free to graze livestock, raise crops, or gather wood, but whose upkeep is the responsibility of no particular person. The ecologist Garrett Hardin has famously described "the tragedy of the commons" as the upshot of this marriage of freedom and irresponsibility. Self-interest leads everyone with access to the commons to take as much as possible, to overgraze or to clear forests, before others do the same. If anyone restrains himself, someone else will take what he has left. What is taken is not renewed, and soon the commons are exhausted.

What strikes me on reading Hardin is that the tragedy he describes is not ineluctable. The depletion of the commons does not just result from innate human nature. The laws of self-interest that move Hardin's analysis are not laws at all. Instead, the tragedy is a cultural and ethical event. It takes place only when we join self-interest with mutual indifference. My investment banker's "iron laws" were at least in part an armored suit that he had donned to

join the great parade of his time. That these destructive principles come from culture rather than nature
does not mean that they are easily changed. It does
mean, however, that honesty requires us to assess
them as the products of human choice. Pretending
that they come to us clothed as laws of science is
dishonest.

In assessing these principles, we need to ask what
they signify for public life, meaning the commons in a
broad sense: the things that we cannot avoid having
in common, and so whose maintenance or neglect
implicates us all. We all rely directly on many elements of the commons: on a legal system that is more
often roughly fair than terribly arbitrary; on the
economy, be it responsible or irresponsible, swift and
efficient or clumsy and makeshift; on the natural
world, the original topic of Hardin's metaphor. The
sense in which we must have these things in common
goes beyond our all depending on them; their upkeep
is a common achievement because we can only maintain them together. Acting well alone, important
though it is, is not enough.

I am not normally an admirer of schemata. However, I believe that it is credible, and also helpful, to
think of what I am calling the commons by conceiving of three ecological systems. The first one is made
up of cultural practices and individual dispositions,
inherited as we take a style of reading from a teacher
or a habit of patience from a parent. In this area of the
commons we develop generosity or greed, thoughtfulness or heedlessness, the capacity for devotion or a

compulsion to self-concern. These are the resources that, among other things, enable us to trust, and to bear the weight of others' trust, even in a time when trust is aggressively discounted. All of this might fairly be called a moral ecology.

Most people contribute to the moral ecology in ways that are not public in any traditional sense, and that we would not want to be public in most senses. Our families and friendships are powerful precisely because they are intimate. Making them "political," devoting them to the strictures of a cause, movement, or state, is often a form of violence. However, these personal practices are common so far as we recognize that in them we sustain or despoil a shared stock of the qualities that enable people to live well together. When a parent, a friend, or a lover harms someone who has trusted him, or acts as a coward after letting another's courage rest with him, or simply acquiesces to some setting that he does not believe to be good, he robs from the other person's capacity to trust, to dare, or to act in conscience. In doing so, he also weakens the other's power ever to teach another person to act well rather than badly.

So our contribution to the moral ecology is mainly personal; yet it is most likely to be good when we think of it in relation to the commons. This is not simple, but it is more nearly possible when it is most necessary. Unless we are especially attentive, we tend to notice the moral ecology only when it fails. Commonplace goodness does not move us much, until we have been squarely confronted with commonplace badness. The more common badness becomes, the more keenly we appreciate goodness. The more we encounter small failings in these common things, the more likely we may be to attend to them as common.

More straightforward, and also more traditionally public, is the second set of commons: the political and civic institutions that create and enforce laws, shape economies, and maintain communities. Without these common things, a good deal that is intensely personal would not be possible, or would take a very different form. Political institutions are the source of a good deal of our security, however imperfect. More often than not, good politics defends and even advances liberty. Often it is indispensable to acting responsibly: to establishing intelligent environmental laws, trying to make real education possible for everybody, and addressing the condition of the poorest neighborhoods and rural regions.

Our neglect of political institutions is the source of much of our private insecurity. The decay of public services that leads ambitious young people to seek escape from them is in good part a product of politics. The upward spiral of imprisonment rates, driven by long mandatory sentences and abetted by a burgeoning private prison industry, is a divisive and alarming gift from politics to all of us. The decline of personal privacy is the product of a politics at once inquisitorial toward suspicious characters and indifferent to the small inconveniences of everyone else.

So far as people other than the very wealthy can affect politics, they generally do so through the institutions of civic life. Whether supporting a candidate or arguing against a dangerous proposal, people act mainly through circles already established: neighborhood associations, unions, professional groups, networks of friends and acquaintances drawn together by common interests. Political work expands, reshapes, and sometimes splinters these connections; but only rarely does it forge them out of nothing. We depend on political decisions for a great deal that is good or bad in our lives and others'. We join in the decision between good and bad mainly on the strength of connections that are not strictly political, but broadly civic. The more we neglect these connections, the less able we are to affect the balance of bad and good that we all inhabit.

The third set of commons is the natural world on which we all depend. It is set off against what is human and cultural, the inarticulate ground of our loquacious existence. However, the well-being of the natural ecology is interwoven with the social and moral. The rise of the environment as one of the main concerns of political debate is only a small reminder that politics is essentially caught up with the decision between stewardship and degradation. So far, there is no way other than politics to decide for or against strip-mining or clear-cutting national forests. Although they have often been disappointing, only national and local governments have even the theoretical power to slow the buildup of greenhouse gases, to guide development that relies less on the automobile and more on public transport, and so on as far as one cares to imagine.

The natural world is equally dependent on the health of the moral ecology. In the end wise environmental behavior is personal behavior. However elaborately our decisions are caught up in the politics and economy in which we move, they are finally personal. It is always one person who buys a product, starts a car, or chooses a career. Environmental responsibility belongs to the moral ecology as much as to the political and civic commons, and both of those can be responsible only if they answer to environmental strictures. None of these can be kept whole if they are thought of separately.

There is another sense in which we are all implicated in the commons, which is a matter not of direct dependence, but of that archaic concept, honor. What is done in the public's name is done in *our* name, every one of us, whether we like it or not. An economy in which we participate is *our* economy, and we cannot disavow responsibility for its depredations. As participants in an irresponsible economy or citizens of a nation with a legal system rife with injustice, we are necessarily less responsible than we might be—or ought to be. Just as intelligence or personality cannot be achieved in isolation, responsibility does not permit itself to be made a mainly personal affair. The paradox of responsibility is that it makes us at once more and less the masters of our own lives. By acknowledging our dependence, we make it our own, and the real character of our lives ceases to be alien to us. However, recognizing our dependence on things that we cannot ever control, we grant that our power declines in proportion to the increase of our responsibility. It is an unsettling proportion, but it has the advantage of being real.

In all, this idea of the commons confounds the distinction between public and private things by attending to what is common in each. We might say that a public act is defined less by where it takes place—a voting booth or courthouse versus a shopping mall, for instance—than by its intent. A public act aims at the upkeep of the commons. Understood in this way, public work embraces a spectrum that begins at one extreme with electoral politics and civil service, passes through public defenders' and prosecutors' offices, continues through activist organizations and unions, newspapers and television networks, and companies that manufacture their products responsibly and reinvest in their communities, and ends in families that raise their children with affection and attention, do not buy what they do not need or genuinely want, and turn at least some of their attention to the rest of the spectrum. Of course, public work also includes the failure of any of these: corrupt politics and courts, vindictive prosecutors and indifferent defenders, shoddy and sensationalistic journalism, and families that turn entirely inward, for their own pleasure or unhappiness.

Most good work includes some element of public concern. This is apparent in the practice of the devoted doctor, the lawyer who works with integrity, or the journalist who serves truth and her consort, lucidity. We could not go on if there were not many people willing to perform these professions well. Witness the political failures of nations with a corrupt or impotent press, let alone the public-health disasters of countries without doctors. Closer to home, consider whether a rich and democratic country could be healthy with a population composed exclusively of plastic surgeons, gossip columnists, and unscrupulous tax attorneys, or whether such work is possible only because others maintain the obligations of their professions and the institutions that their work upholds.

This public quality is not restricted to professionals. Public life cannot maintain its seriousness if it is just a morally satisfying bauble for the wealthy and accomplished. To take the simplest case—the oldest and still the most fundamental of our dependences—there is the kind of farming that ensures that farming will be possible in the same place five thousand years later, and the kind that exhausts soil and aquifers and starts the path to desert. Farming done well and conscientiously is partly public work. So is the work of teachers who elicit insights and inculcate habits of thought and discussion, and so contribute to the reflection and debate of the next generation. A tradesman who upholds and passes on the standards of his craft makes the same sort of contribution. A bad carpenter, a second-rate writer or editor, or an indifferent teacher contributes to a culture that is thoughtless, semi-literate, slapdash, and unreliable in its sentences and its structures alike. People who do necessary work well help to keep this quiet disaster at bay. We all rely, directly or indirectly, on such people and endeavors, and are afflicted by the others. The proportion between the two is partly ours to set.

Confounding the distinction between public and private is appropriate, for this distinction is confounded in reality by the elaborate interconnection among the several commons. Professions are performed only by individuals, and the integrity of professional practice is not easily isolated from the integrity of a whole character, the habits of valuation, judgment, and perception that guide a person through the world. The Free Agent of *Fast Company*, Tom Peters's self-brander, or the ideal reader of *Wired* is not going to become a lawyer committed to public service, a devoted general practitioner, or a responsible farmer; if he does, the professional choice will be a kind of conversion. As we gradually cultivate one or another set of characteristics in ourselves, we make ourselves fit or unfit for particular kinds of work.

Responsibility and Freedom

Only an individual can *think of* herself and her work as containing an element that is inescapably public. This identification does not happen by accident. Although it may be facilitated by them, it is not brought about by national policies or the exhortations of professional bodies. If it were ever ensured by unthinking tradition, it is not now: today a person belongs to a tradition only inasmuch as she seeks it out, aligns herself with it, and puts herself in its line of tutelage.

This is why the nature of the commons has changed in a most important way. I have been using a language that may suggest inherited obligation—inescapably carrying responsibility for the well-being of a place and for the acts of a political community. Yet inherited obligation is a thing of the past. John Locke, the founding thinker of modern political society and especially of American politics, held that because political obligation was based on the free consent of citizens, no state could be legitimate that denied its members the right to leave it. That idea has not left us since. Many of the defining figures of modern political reflection cast the same conviction in the distinctly American mold of Thoreau. They are inner emigrés, whose first loyalty is to conscience or to some particular, freely chosen, and often dissenting moral community.

Moreover, a nation of immigrants is founded on the prerogative to leave something behind in favor of something else. It begins with the refusal of inherited duty. It is no surprise that American Catholics are selective to the point of Protestantism in their reception of church teachings, or that Americans are "born again" with a frequency that baffles the populations of other prosperous and educated countries. This practice is a religious analogue to our restless movements and self-inventions. The strain of Jay Gatsby in us runs as far back as Benjamin Franklin, an emi-

nently self-made man who practiced his artless manner and crafted his naivete as scrupulously as anyone
before or after him. We honor only what we have chosen, and sometimes only what we have made.

These experiences and attitudes are cornerstones
of our identity. We could not be rid of them. Obligation to the commons, then, requires not the return of
hereditary obligation but the self-discipline of liberty.
It is the mark of our freedom that we can ignore any
tradition and refuse any loyalty. We are at liberty to
be entirely self-concerned. Our freedom, though, does
not prohibit seriousness of purpose; it may be that
it can come to maturity only by undertaking such
seriousness. With a free, reflective choice to accept
responsibility for some place, to take a role in a political and geographic community, and to answer to
some tradition, we take full responsibility for our
lives. We relinquish boundlessness to acquire form.

I cannot consider this idea without thinking of the
decisive act in the life of my fellow Appalachian Wendell Berry. Berry, an essayist, novelist, poet, teacher,
and farmer, was born in Port Royal, Kentucky, where
his family had farmed for generations. He was a gifted
writer, and after attending a local college went to
Stanford, where what is now the Wallace Stegner Program in Fiction was then simply Wallace Stegner's
program. Berry earned Stegner's admiration. At the
same time, he fell in with a roughly bohemian group
of Stegner's students, including Ken Kesey, author of
One Flew Over the Cuckoo's Nest, who would later
become a literary character of sorts as leader of the

madcap Merry Pranksters in Tom Wolfe's *The Electric Kool-Aid Acid Test*. After Stanford, Berry made his way to Manhattan, where he began teaching at New York University and where his first novel was published to a good reception. He seemed, so far as can be judged in the uncertain trade of writing, to be on his way.

Then he left. Or, as it seemed to him, he returned. He moved with his wife to a farm in Port Royal, where he has lived ever since. He writes there, works his crops with draft horses, and has long taught English at the University of Kentucky. On first returning, he has admitted, he could not ignore the admonitions of his literary elders in New York that he would find Kentucky a cultural and intellectual desert. He was prepared to struggle against isolation, ennui, and the sluggishness of parochial thought. Instead, he found a quickening and refinement of his sensibility. He discovered a new relation to the place: "Before, it had been mine by coincidence or accident; now it was mine by choice." With that freely assumed bond came a newly keen awareness of the region: "I walked over it, looking, listening, smelling, touching, alive to it as never before. I listened to the talk of my kinsmen and neighbors as I had never done, alert to their knowledge of the place, and to the qualities and energies of their speech. I began more seriously than ever to learn the names of things—the wild plants and animals, the natural processes, the local places—and to articulate my observations and memories."

Berry describes our intense awareness of things that we have knowingly made a part of ourselves. We can be casual toward accidental circumstances, and indifferent to what we know to be transient; but we cannot, with any honesty, neglect to attend to what has become forever a portion of ourselves. This attention is not just the pleasurable exercise of observing a place well; it also reveals the sometimes painful burden of having accepted complicity in all the wrongs and harms of the place. Reflecting on his return, Berry recalls: "When I lived in other places I looked on their evils with the curious eye of a traveler; I was not responsible for them; it cost me nothing to be a critic, for I had not been there long, and I did not feel that I would stay. But here, now that I am both native and citizen, there is no immunity to what is wrong." To choose to circumscribe oneself, to take responsibility for one's web of dependences, is both enriching and demanding. It is a surrender of immunity. But the immunity is a superficial kind, fantastic and, in the end, untenable. It rests on the refusal to acknowledge reliances, or the refusal to take reliance as a source of obligation.

Since his return, Berry has been an eloquent exponent of staying over leaving, fidelity over fecklessness, and carefully drawn limits against boundless ambition and desire. His work celebrates farming and marriage as the inner terms of concentric circles of devotion and obligation, where "desire and necessity are one." He is America's most articulate source of caution against heedless self-seeking. Yet it is of first importance, in his own life and in a proper understanding of his work, that his "necessity" is freely chosen, undertaken out of a young man's love that came to fullness in the place and the work that it had selected. This is the nature of obligation today. It may have sources in birth, but its authority comes in choice. Responsibility begins in the twofold act of accepting one body of duties and tasks and forsaking the pleasures of all others.

Our liberty means unprecedented power to neglect the questions that tradition addresses, and that responsibility to any commons relies upon: What am I doing, and for what? What is the meaning of my work, and what are its purposes? What attachments—to people, to places, to principles—am I working to maintain, and why? Whose well-being is in my hands, and in whose hands is mine? We cannot answer those questions in solitude, without the history that brings us to where we are and the tradition that poses the questions; yet it is often alone that we begin to select the place and the terms that will form our answer. The decision between responsibility and neglect rests with each of us. The circle of responsible work moves through the commons and the individual. It is in the individual that it can be decisively broken. Today it is the individual, moving from liberty into freely chosen circumscription, who can make it whole.

Coming into the Public

Thinking about public work in terms of responsibility leads, in a roundabout way, back to politics and political institutions. Although we are inclined to forget it, these rank high among the things on which we rely. For Tocqueville, whether we could avoid forgetting would decide what Americans made of their democracy. Although he was a great student of temperament, he held that indifference to politics was not just a matter of disposition. Instead, it was a cognitive error, a bald mistake about where one's proper concerns lay.

Tocqueville's great fear was that Americans, relatively prosperous and relatively free, would fall into the illusion that "each man holds his fate in his own hands." Withdrawing into wholly private concerns, "each man is thrown back on himself alone," and anything that individuals could not accomplish in solitude would fall to bureaucrats. Americans would forget how to govern themselves. They would forget how to be free.

Because Tocqueville enjoys great cachet, he has been posthumously recruited by scholars and critics from both left and right. For conservatives, he warns against the welfare state, portraying big, centralized government as sapping civic energies. For liberals and those further to the left, Tocqueville describes the power of selfish individualism to draw people out of public life and make them less, not more free.

Both are right, but neither is right alone. Tocqueville, like many great figures of the past, encompasses and confounds our contemporary divisions. He thought that both individualism and unthinking reliance on government were deformations of culture and personality, and he believed that they were inextricably interwoven with each other. In his view, the illusion of self-sufficiency always meant surrendering a portion of responsibility for one's own life to some other, larger body—and, at the same time, abdicating from participation in that body. As we became more superficially independent, we would lose the real liberty of having a hand in shaping our circumstances—which in turn shape us. The result would look at its gentlest like a nursing-home version of social democracy, but it would be born from a lack, not an excess, of solidarity.

Tocqueville's conception emphatically places politics within the idea of public work. It presents politics as essentially public, in the sense that I have been defending. This is a politics of equal parts transformation and maintenance. Such a politics does not make the same promises that Promethean politics does. It does not so readily provide the cornerstone of moral identity. It cannot save our actions from futility by the redemption of its eventual triumph. It does not alter the founding elements of human experience. Instead, it is an unending acknowledgment of those, a dogged exercise in grappling with them.

We have a model for the contemporary renewal of this idea in the last decade of Central European history. In Poland and the former Czechoslovakia, some of our time's political heroes have undergone the transition from revolutionary drama to democratic politics, and helping their countries to make the same passage. They are the veterans of Czechoslovakia's Charter 77 organization and Poland's Solidarity trade union and Workers' Defense Committees (KOR). Their story provides one picture of what a renewed public politics might be.

The choice of Central Europe for a discussion of American politics must seem curious. However, that region has earned a place in the imagination of people who would like to believe in the possible goodness of politics despite the disappointment of recent years. In years of opposition to Communism, the dissidents of Central Europe developed a rich idea of the moral import of politics and turned that idea into a political program that, in the magic year 1989, seemed to triumph across their region. In that time they appeared to know better than anyone else alive how politics could be made to matter. Moreover, they spoke back to Americans the phrases of our founding political myths, with a conviction that has not recently been heard here. They were revolutionaries in the name of individual liberty, democratic government, and the rule of law. They invoked Tocqueville, James Madison, and Adam Smith. At the center of their thought was the conviction that civil society, a dense network of voluntary organizations and public participation, was necessary to maintain the freedom they hoped to achieve.

In the United States, this is the easily ignored stuff of political piety. We have nearly forgotten that anyone would live for it. Yet dissidents such as Czechoslovakia's Vaclav Havel and Poland's Adam Michnik showed themselves willing to suffer imprisonment, sometimes undergo beatings, and in a few cases die for our pieties. They made their principles the centerpiece of a theater of political heroism. Since their victory in 1989, they have been working their way back toward the less heroic work of ordinary politics, and have shown how some of their old devotion can survive in new and undramatic work. At their best, they show how public work remains urgent after it ceases being magical.

In 1981, responding to nationwide strikes, Poland's Communist government declared martial law and imprisoned thousands of members of Solidarity without trial. Michnik, scion of a Jewish Warsaw family and by training a historian, was among those imprisoned longest. When his cell was opened three years later, Michnik refused to leave. He was fighting, he said, not for his own freedom but for political liberty and the rule of law, and those had come no closer since he had been thrown in jail. He wanted vindication by trial. Until then, he preferred to wait in the cramped room that he shared with ordinary criminals.

Michnik's gesture captured the extraordinary moral power of dissident politics. The founding idea of Central European dissent was that truth and integrity were the greatest political weapons. It was an idea posed in answer to grim conditions. The dissidents faced a public life drained of high purpose. Communism had won over some of the brightest and most morally sensitive members of the anti-Nazi resistance in Poland and the prewar progressive movement in Czechoslovakia, but well before the 1970s the Communist Party, the sole occupant of the region's public sphere, was corrupt, repressive, and populated by opportunists.

Public life was not only corrupt; it was also unreal. The state-controlled media spoke the language of propaganda, denouncing enemies in headlines and misrepresenting everything from farm production statistics to geopolitics. Private experience contradicted much of what was publicly declared, but announcing that experience, making it public, was a crime. So politics and public life came apart from ordinary reality, and people inhabited one world even as they were addressed and expected to answer in the language of another. All this was not only unsettling, but also quietly humiliating. In public speech and action, citizens were required to betray their own knowledge and convictions. If they gave up on the public world altogether, as most did, they retreated into a private life hemmed in on all sides by the political and economic power of the Communist Party.

The centerpiece of Central European dissent was the aim of recovering personal integrity and public truth with a single gesture. The dissidents' chief instrument would be neither the bullet nor the ballot, but the truthful sentence. Barred from practicing their professions, often imprisoned, they persisted in a kind of civic testimony, the declaration of principled defiance that in itself disrupted a political culture built on acquiescence to lies. Havel wrote of a fictional grocer whom he imagined refusing one day to place a piece of state propaganda in his shop window: "By breaking the rules of the game, he has disrupted the game as such. He has exposed it as a mere game. He has shattered the world of appearances."

Shattering public appearances meant reclaiming personal integrity. Dissent was an attitude to the world, a deportment that many saw as an honest person's only way of avoiding humiliation in a regime that compromised everything it touched. Michnik's most powerful essays from that period address this situation with pleas for resistance in the face of seeming hopelessness. Faced with interrogation by security forces, Michnik wrote in a letter from his cell, "You find yourself engaged in a philosophical debate with them about the meaning of your life. . . . You are engaged in the argument of Giordano Bruno with the Inquisitor . . . of Carl von Ossietzky with the blond Gestapo officer. . . . You score a victory not when you win power, but when you remain faithful to yourself." Michnik made good these principles in 1984, when he refused to leave his cell. This personal certainty sustained the dissidents, even when other kinds of victory seemed unattainable.

The political victories of 1989 changed all that. In a flash, Adam Michnik was Deputy Michnik, parliamentary representative from Warsaw. Vaclav Havel was president of Czechoslovakia, soon to split, over his objections, into Slovakia and the Czech Republic. With power came new divisions, and both countries' leading dissident organizations were soon splintered. Within a few years, most of the dissidents were out of politics.

Under communism, the dissidents had presented the regime with a curious mirror image of itself. Authoritarian politics extended into every sphere of life. The dissidents' response was to make high-minded politics into a form of opposition that was also a form of life. They were perhaps the last serious people for whom politics fulfilled the promise that had, ironically, been one of the great attractions of communism: providing a basic orientation to the world, answering the inescapable questions "What shall I do?" and "How shall I live?" An extraordinary moral clarity crystallized in the politics of dissent.

Ordinary democratic politics has denied that clarity to its Central European participants. It has proven a politics of compromise, ambiguity, and almost inescapable ambivalence. Even when an issue seems clear, no party is without its contemptible motives or dubious alliances, no program lacks worrisome elements. Above all, the programs of democratic politics are answers to specifically political questions. They do not readily give moral clarity, the elusive quality of "meaning," to lives that do not already have it. With the coming of democracy, dissidents for whom politics had been irresistible because it was the only way to clarity in a befogged society now found governance a source of confusion and frustration. Politics had become home to what they had worked all along to avoid: banality and compromise.

Havel is the tragic hero of this transition. His moral charisma and elegant prose have enabled him to retain the admiration of most Czechs, when other dissidents are largely forgotten. However, his calls to truth and honesty have been received more as homilies than as serious proposals. He could not stop the division of Czechoslovakia or the campaign of political retribution that exposed and humiliated collaborators with the old regime, and his office has become chiefly a ceremonial and hortatory one. Many Czech observers perceive him as bitterly disappointed by a democratic politics that muddles in demagoguery, self-interest, and game-playing. He saw Jericho fall, seemingly at a trumpet blast, and now finds his countrymen indifferent to the same note.

Havel's phrase for the political practice that "shattered the world of appearances" was "living in truth," and the perception that the dissidents stood for truth against a regime of falsehood was widespread. Michnik asserted that Poland's Communist state was administered with "a language that has lies and blackmail at its core," and Havel insisted that "the main pillar of the system is living a lie." Now it seemed that the commitment to truth as the heart of politics could make sense only in a struggle against a government that rested on falsehood. After the achievement of democracy, facts became less embattled and relatively less precious than in the authoritarian era, while the moral issues up for dispute often lacked obvious answers. Where dissident politics should go, and whether its spirit could survive at all, was poignantly unclear.

Integrity and Doubt

When clarity fails the first temptation is to look for new certainties. Yet political certainty is rife with danger. The best warning against its excesses comes from the example of those who have tried to hold on to it where it is no longer possible. Antoni Macerewicz, a KOR veteran, parliamentary deputy, and publisher of a small, Catholic newspaper, believes that Poland is not yet free. For him, "The essence of Polish oppression was Communist occupation." Today the former Communists, who dominated the old state industries and financial structures, have done well in the often corrupt privatization process or have used political ties to advance their financial speculation. At the same time, they have often kept control of local governments. Macerewicz does not stipulate how these old Communists should be eliminated from the new economy, but his language suggests that a crusade of some kind is required to make Poland whole. In its proper role, the nation is "a guardian of Christian civilization," which is embattled in the decadent West. When pressed, Macerewicz will say that Poland stands at the crux of "the problem of white civilization—Europe, North America, and Australia—

facing billions of people with completely different values."

At the core of their motives Macerewicz and his allies have a desire for the old certainties, a time when evil seemed to lie in one place alone, and good belonged to those who opposed it. By making the conflict between authoritarianism and democracy a prelude to the crisis of Western civilization, they have preserved the certainty of their moral compasses, but perhaps at the cost of what the late scholar Isaiah Berlin used to call "the sense of reality."

It is revealing that those who have the most claim on the old certainties have also been most adamant in insisting that they no longer hold. Michnik today insists that the moral absolutism that accompanies antitotalitarianism has no place in democratic politics. Instead, entering into democracy "requires overcoming the contempt for imperfection." In the same vein, Havel has made it one of his themes that no one was wholly untouched by complicity in the old regime, that "we are all guilty." Both he and Michnik have opposed identifying and purging old Communists. For them integrity has become a more complicated matter than ever before. Both have concluded that self-scrutiny and forgiveness are now its first requirements.

The Political and the Public

The disappointments of ordinary politics were especially keen for the dissidents because Michnik, Havel, and others had imagined that their work displayed a model not just for dissent but also for renewing the politics of a democratic country. By night, sometimes in hiding, they had created a small and beleaguered free society within their unfree nations. KOR and Solidarity, which at its peak included ten million members, were efforts to develop an independent civil society where not just a few intellectuals, but ordinary men and women could speak and act freely, give and receive mutual aid, and otherwise share in the political community that an authoritarian state denied them. Michnik and other strategists suggested that a sufficiently strong society might induce the state to wither away, in Marx's phrase—but as a way out of, not into communism.

Many dissidents began to see adversarial power politics as a social deformation, and imagined replacing it with a public life of reasoned dialogue and service to a commonly recognized good. They imagined a kind of civic third way, public life with neither the state repression of the East nor the politically indifferent consumer culture of the West. Havel wrote in 1984, "I favor 'antipolitical politics,' that is, politics . . . as one of the ways of seeking and achieving meaningful lives, of protecting them and serving them." Governance, like dissent, could be an essentially moral exercise. Politics would follow from the marriage of moral truth and high motive. Havel called such politics "service to the truth," and leading dissidents across the region came to treasure the idea.

The rapid death of this hope produced despair and extremism. It also drew many dissidents toward a broadened idea of public work. If the expansion of politics into all realms of life under communism had been a distortion, after 1989 bringing all high aspirations into the narrow realm of politics was equally confused. However, many of those aspirations have a place in public life, in institutions and communities that are not properly political but whose health is indispensable to the health of politics.

The first leading dissident to understand this fully was Adam Michnik. In 1990 he joined much of the staff of the leading underground weekly, *Tygodnik Masowsze*, in founding Poland's first legal "opposition" paper, *Gazeta Wyborcza* (Election Paper), whose title recalls its initial mission in that extraordinary year. With the election over, Michnik and his collaborators saw that the opposition press was on its way to becoming obsolete, while a nascently democratic Poland badly needed responsible, nonpartisan media. With Michnik as editor the opposition veterans crafted a daily newspaper that serves as Poland's *New York Times* and *New York Review of Books* rolled into one, and also—not least because of its top-drawer classified and consumer affairs sections— easily maintains the country's highest circulation. The paper has earned a reputation for liberal opinion and objective and scrupulous reportage. Its investigative reporters turn up political and financial scandals with unsettling regularity, while its editors cast a chilly, often sarcastic eye on both nostalgic Communist apologists and would-be anti-Communist crusaders.

Although most have at least one independent, well-edited newspaper, no other post-Communist country has benefited from the level of journalism that *Gazeta Wyborcza* has brought Poland. Ironically, the flamboyant dissident Michnik may have made his largest contribution to Polish democracy in the relatively undramatic work of making the free and independent press a reality. Michnik's Warsaw admirers like to observe that he has simply followed his old principle of pursuing the most difficult and urgent work of his time: overthrow in one period, building-up in another.

Michnik's work today finds echoes across Poland and the Czech Republic. Former dissidents work as journalists and environmental advocates, in local and national nongovernmental organizations, and as teachers and religious leaders. Those who remain in electoral politics are mainly connected with these broader communities, and they are as much emissaries to politics as they are themselves politicians. A representative figure is Jacek Kuron, a tireless Solidarity organizer and close adviser to Solidarity leader Lech Walesa before 1989, who holds a senatorial seat in addition to his chief work as director of a service organization that feeds and educates needy children. As a senator, Kuron works mainly to aid children and Poland's Roma, or gypsies, and refers to himself wryly as "the minister of poverty and hopelessness." For these people, politicians and otherwise, public life is now a matter of maintenance and slow construction, rather than transformation; but when that is the most important work, it is just as necessary as the headier project of revolution was a decade ago.

This species of public commitment has been especially important in Central Europe as an answer to the libertarianism that sprang up there with the revolutions of 1989. Especially in the Czech Republic, where intellectual life had been starved by censorship since the Soviet-led invasion of 1968, the leading alternatives to Marxism among intellectuals were paeans to the unfettered market by Milton Friedman and Friedrich Hayek. Vaclav Klaus, the Czech prime minister, pronounced an inadvertent vulgar Marxism: the free market, permitted to go its own way without government interference, would automatically produce a liberal, democratic culture and cement the rule of law. Klaus made plain his scorn for the idea of "civil society" as a thing apart from the market, expressing ironic puzzlement that anything so ostensibly valuable should be unable to turn a profit.

Now the results of that attitude are becoming clear. Much more even than in troubled Poland, economic privatization has gone off track in the Czech Republic because democratic control has failed. Big industries have been handed off to well-connected investors. Politically powerful individuals have bought controlling shares of former state companies, then funneled assets to their own corporations and left the old companies shells; under Czech law, minority stockholders have no recourse against this kind of economic cannibalism. At the same time, Prague, a city of a million people, now houses over 1,200 private security companies, many of them effectively debt-collection agencies: the courts and police are too inefficient and corrupt to enforce either private contracts or criminal law, and law enforcement has become something of a private commodity. In turn, the whole mess has produced a class of wealthy and influential figures with no interest in effective political or economic reform: corruption engenders its own defenders. In 1998, slow economic growth slipped into contraction, and more and more Czechs began to wonder whether Margaret Thatcher–style free-market policies had been an appropriate import for a nascent democracy.

Their doubt confirms one of the most important of the dissidents' surviving convictions. In the wake of an era when it has been common to hope for too much from politics, the greater and more dangerous temptation is now to hope for too little from public life. Politics often registers as distasteful, prurient, and, in the libertarian fantasy of a wholly private life, superfluous. The dissidents of Europe never had the privilege of developing the last delusion. They could never doubt that the health of public life was intimately related to the well-being of everyone in their countries, and that politics and the broader idea of *public* work depended intimately on each other. Even if they have not invented a new kind of politics, they have maintained some of their old clarity and vitality in their current work. The rupture of 1989 is striking; but just as impressive, on examination, is how many motives remain intact on both sides of that divide.

The Meeting of the Twain

"Banality is an achievement." This phrase, from a KOR veteran who now writes for *Gazeta Wyborcza*, captures much of the paradox of politics in Europe today. It is an instructive paradox for politics everywhere. The liberation of private life from politics is one of the great attainments of a moderately free society. Communist repression touched the dissidents most intimately by denying them the liberty to write freely, to speak their minds, to pursue their careers. The intellectual freedom that they fought for means precisely the freedom to be unpolitical. Former underground editors recall with delighted relief the disentanglement of professional and political standards that became possible after 1989, when they once again felt free to exclude bad poetry from their pages no matter how staunch the author's democratic convictions. The freedom to distinguish between good and bad poetry, regardless of politics, can sometimes be as compelling a recommendation as any for liberal democracy.

It is the mark of Central Europe's recent achievements that the region no longer inspires much histrionics, or has need of much heroism. Yet a political achievement cannot be taken for granted. It is always either a continuing accomplishment or an eroding one. It requires the sustenance of unheroic work. In keeping up one's share of that work, it is instructive to recall that political principles can touch women and men intimately enough to sustain what seems likely to be a lost cause. They can be as concrete as the desire to avoid prison or to pursue one's career, as universal as the impulse to live in dignity rather than in prostration. For the dissidents of Central Europe, acting on these principles was a way, first individually, then socially, of reclaiming their lives.

This is especially important because the dissidents' drama was also, in a real and conscious way, our drama. They relied absolutely on values that in the past two centuries have had their symbolic home— and a share of their actual existence—in America. They explored the outermost limits of those values as a foundation for contemporary revolution, for political heroism, and for the orientation and sustenance of the individual soul. If, in the end, they gave up a good portion of their aspirations, they also managed to keep more than most Americans have recently hoped to gain.

The public work that the dissidents continue to practice is a way of confronting certain unchanging features of the human predicament. Foremost among these is the persistence of what might be called the sources of evil. These are greed and fear, and the willingness to seek and misuse power to serve both; the passion for self-righteousness, to stand, entirely good, against those who are nothing but bad; the pleasure and psychic relief of cruelty; and the capacity for sheer, willful destruction. They exist alongside generosity, courage, modesty, kindness, and the impulses of care. Together, they produce the founding paradox of good politics: people can be improved, but not beyond the need for one another and for common institutions that fix our best commitments and constrain and redirect our worst impulses.

Heroism and banality have a curious coexistence in public work, and it is often salutary to concentrate on the latter. Still, there is no wisdom in forgetting that both exist, or in neglecting the more demanding of the two. The truth is that the possibility of a decent life is partly an achievement of political and public institutions, and that ignoring these is the surest way to hasten their decline. We serve that truth by working in a public life that cannot make us whole, but may help us to stay together. Central Europe's dissidents have the right, if anyone has, to issue that reminder. We have the freedom to take it up or ignore it.

CHAPTER FOUR

The Law of the Land: Political Choice and Attentiveness

But the mountain falls and crumbles away, and the rock is removed from its place; the waters wear away the stones; the torrents wash away the soil of the earth; so thou destroyest the hope of man.

—Job 14:18–19

IN 1996, Secretary of the Interior Bruce Babbitt visited Hobet 21, one of West Virginia's largest mountaintop-removal strip mines. He arrived at a place where mountaintops across thousands of acres had been dynamited and bulldozers had pushed the shattered earth into the surrounding valleys, leaving a plateau of shale and clay. Some grass grew on the site, and few tough locust trees stood as much as twelve feet high.

Babbitt arrived by helicopter, crossing rugged green hills to reach the dull, uneven plain of the mine. He stepped behind a podium hastily erected in an otherwise empty field, surveyed the ground before him, and made an astonishing pronouncement. He said, "This is in some ways a better landscape than it was before. It's a much more diverse landscape, a savannah of fields and forests coming back. It is in some ways closer to the landscape that existed here a thousand years ago than the unmined landscape." He ended by referring to "the miracle that we see upon this ground today." Coal companies have taken to using his phrases in full-page newspaper advertisements defending mountaintop removal.

What Babbitt said is not only false, but dangerously absurd. It was contradicted by everything he saw around him, everything he must have seen on his flight to the mine, everything the most ignorant naturalist knows about the growth of landforms. Whatever one thinks of the virtues of tough-grassed plains, installing them in Appalachia is not an act of restoration. Babbitt was announcing a fantasy that took flight, just for a moment, on his prominence and position, and has been kept aloft by its usefulness to mining companies. In that moment, he spoke as a man impregnable to the reality around him.

Babbitt's sentences are more representative than aberrant. The overwhelming quality of much public talk is its air of unreality. That is a part of what the ironist and the political cynic have noted. It contributes to skepticism that public speech can ever touch reality, and that public acts can preserve or better it. Unreal things are not very important, unless a person is delusional, and so it is not surprising that this unreal quality exists alongside a widespread idea that public life is superfluous. It is one of the conceits of our time that politics and law might have their sole purpose in the administration of free markets. This is the idea of politicians who would rest policy on the calculation of economic costs and benefits alone, and of judges and legal scholars who argue that laws should never do more than enforce private agreements. It is the doctrine of international free traders certain that prosperity lies on the other side of borders opened to the unlimited exchange of money and goods.

This attitude is attractive because it is reassuring. It suggests that public questions have one right answer, the one that will make markets work well. This means that those questions need not really be public, but can be entrusted to well-trained managers of prosperity. With this conviction fixed, we can afford indifference to other putatively public matters. The fatuous and unreal air of politicians is a small annoyance so long as the real decisions lie with the famously sober Federal Reserve Board. With our collective business in good hands, we are free to enjoy our private comforts. This is a soft version of the imagined future that haunted Tocqueville.

It is also a wrong view. Every law and each political choice is in part a judgment about the sort of country we will inhabit and the sort of lives we will lead. There is no escaping this fact, only the possibility of evading it for a period, as we are now trying to do. At best, ignoring necessity is reckless. At worst, it is destructive.

I do not know another way of communicating this than by telling a story from West Virginia. The landscape of that place remains my mind's homeland. When I think of responsibility or foolishness, preservation or destruction, generosity or greed, they take the forms of Appalachia. They come to me as green slopes and shattered hills, good and poor farms, faces firm with practiced concern, contorted with outrage, or slack and ruddy with indifference.

In West Virginia, the great themes run through coal. Glistening black carbon formed from the beds of ancient swamps and shallow seas, coal seems foreign to a time whose hopes hang by thin filaments of silicon. It is mythic stuff: the rock that burns, the flammable guts of mountains. Coal is the gift of the Mesozoic to the industrial age, and we can easily imagine that it has nothing to do with us. But in West Virginia, its power remains elemental.

The Death of Mountains

Driving his battered sedan through Blair, West Virginia, a cigarette dangling between thin fingers, James Weekley passes among ghosts. "There stood three houses," he says, gesturing at a flat, grassy area below the narrow, two-lane road, "and across the creek were two more. They sold a year back, then they burned." Five years ago, this small town, strung along a creek bottom between two mountains, had stores, an elementary school, and twice as many families as the eighty who now live here. Then the Dal-Tex coal company began strip-mining Blair Mountain. Since then, the community has been darkened by dust storms, battered by flying rock, and shaken by dynamite blasts. Every month more residents sell their homes to the company and move out. When the job is done, not much will be left of the town or the mountain.

These hills are some of the oldest in the world. They lie to the west of the great Appalachian chain, the line of north-south ridges that once stood higher than the Rockies and are now worn to gentle folds whose highest reaches press toward five thousand feet. From the western edge of those mountains to the Ohio River once ran the Allegheny Plateau, an upland of clay, sandstone, shale, and coal. Blair Mountain and the rest of Logan County were worn into the plateau by meandering streams. From a high place, the land has the idly patterned quality of melting honeycomb. The slopes are forbiddingly steep, the ridges narrow, and the streambed bottoms cramped and shadowed by encroaching hillsides.

This high country was used as a hunting ground by the Mound Builder cultures of the Ohio Valley, whose settlements followed the Kanawha River well into what is now West Virginia. If there had ever been lasting homes here, though, their last traces had disappeared before the first white settlers pressed north from the Carolinas after the American Revolution.

They were Scots and Scots-Irish, and their names remain here, mixed with those of the Greeks and Italians who came later to work the mines. A name like Carlos Gore, equal parts Latin and Celtic, is not uncommon here. Near the turn of this century, many of them sold the rights to the minerals beneath their land for a pittance to speculators employed by East Coast landholding companies.

During the first decades of the century, mining exploded in southern Appalachia. In the camps miners rented houses owned by the coal companies, bought their tools and clothes from company supply stores, and purchased food and household supplies with scrip, crudely stamped coins issued by the companies in lieu of real money. The mines were unsafe, precautions were uneven and inadequate, and death from cave-ins and suffocation was common.

In the 1920s, organizers from the United Mine Workers of America (UMWA) led unionization strikes across the region. The company bosses responded by hiring strikebreakers from the Pinkerton and Baldwin-Felts detective agencies. Miners and strikebreakers fought scattered gun battles throughout southern West Virginia in a bloody period that has come down in stories as the Mine Wars. In 1922, after the imprisonment of Sid Hatfield, a county sheriff who had thrown his power behind local strikers, ten thousand armed miners marched from Charleston into the heart of the coalfields. They met a citizen militia and band of strikebreakers at Blair Mountain, and fought a three-day gun battle that ended only when

President Warren G. Harding called in a National Guard division from Ohio. The miners disbanded. The union finally came ten years later, when UMWA president John L. Lewis organized Appalachia with the support of the Roosevelt administration.

Coal mining is an old story in Appalachia. So is conflict between citizens and mining companies. The new boom, the one that has claimed Blair, is driven by mountaintop removal. Coal companies have strip-mined five hundred square miles of West Virginia since 1981. In 1995–97, the state's Division of Environmental Protection (DEP) authorized 27,000 acres of new mountaintop mining, after permitting just under 10,000 acres throughout the 1980s. The largest existing mine alone will cover perhaps 20,000 acres before it closes early in the next century, and mines on the same scale are becoming more common. Valley fills have buried 469 miles of streams in five southwestern watersheds, and an estimated 700 miles across the state.

Coal Power

The rise of mountaintop removal displays the power of the market. The coal industry is enjoying a huge, largely jobless boom. Coal produces more than half of American electricity, and its cost per unit of energy is lower than that of any other fossil fuel. U.S. coal production went over a billion tons for the first time in 1990, and has stayed there in each year since 1994. The average coal miner has tripled his production per man-hour in the past decade, in a time when productivity gains in the whole economy have hardly passed 2 percent per year.

Those gains came with wholesale changes in the coal industry. Although dust-coated miners in headlamps still emerge every evening from mines in West Virginia, Kentucky, and Pennsylvania, their numbers have been dwindling for decades. Increasingly they are replaced by bulldozers, explosives, and the Goliaths of the coalfields, earthmoving machines that stand twenty stories high and can pick up 130 tons of dirt and rock with a bite of their shovels. Coal employment has declined by half nationwide in the past decade, and by a third in West Virginia. In 1948, before the advent of strip-mining, West Virginia alone was home to more miners than are employed in the entire nation today.

The heart of the new coal industry is strip-mining—and the most efficient form of stripping is mountaintop removal. Strip-mining now accounts for 62 percent of U.S. coal production, and one-third of West Virginia's. Nationally, the average strip miner produces three times as much coal as his underground counterpart.

Other trends push Appalachia's coal operators toward stripping. The price of coal has fallen steadily from more than $30 per ton in 1981 to just over $20 in 1998, increasing the pressure to dig more and faster. Western miners benefit from thick, easily accessible coal seams, tightening pressure on the thin seams and steep mountains of the East. Finally, the 1990

Clean Air Act directs power plants to use coal low in sulfur, because high-sulfur coal is the chief cause of acid rain. Southern West Virginia is rich in low-sulfur coal, often distributed in thin horizontal veins, like icing in a layer cake, through hundreds of vertical feet of sandstone, earth, and shale—difficult to mine by traditional methods, but easily accessible by mountain-top removal. Appalachia's mining companies face pressure from every side to tear down the mountains.

A Landscape Under Law

Yet the inexorable logic of the market does not arise of itself. It is deeply entwined with law, and that law in turn is inseparable from the ways that money and power have run their own writ on the Appalachian landscape. To begin with, mining companies are not supposed to be conducting mountaintop removal at will. Strip-mining in the United States is governed by a 1977 federal law, the Surface Mining Control and Reclamation Act (SMCRA), called "SMACK-ra" by those who work with it. The act was passed after six years of congressional battles and vetoes by President Gerald Ford in 1975 and 1976. Its real origins, though, lie in eastern Kentucky, where strip-mining exploded without meaningful regulation in the 1960s. People whose property lay over coal owned by mining companies found their fields, woods, and family cemeteries destroyed without recompense.

In incidents that became folk legends, elderly mountaineers threw themselves to the ground before approaching bulldozers, sometimes shaming the strippers into withdrawing. Others broke into the dynamite sheds of stripping sites and used the stolen explosives to sabotage bulldozers and backhoes. In the same period, Kentucky lawyer Harry Caudill won national attention with powerful histories of the coal industry's presence in his state, including the bleak, elegiac masterpiece *Night Comes to the Cumberlands*.

By 1972, coalitions of local residents, young participants in Volunteers in Service to America (VISTA), and members of the region's nascent environmental movement were agitating across Appalachia for an end to stripping. Then a dam built of mining detritus burst, sending a wall of black water down Buffalo Creek in Logan County, West Virginia. One hundred and twenty-five people died in the flood, and no serious person could any longer pretend that stripping's only cost was a scarred landscape.

Strip-mining legislation had already been introduced in Congress by Ken Hechler, a flamboyant, idealistic representative from southern West Virginia. Hechler had a reputation for straight, sometimes uncomfortable talk and for absolute integrity. A graduate of Swarthmore and Columbia and a former professor of politics at Princeton, he referred to "justice and equity" without bombast or irony; avoiding excessive self-seriousness, he cultivated the habit of breaking into parodic song during speeches. He earned grudging recognition as an effective legislator when he successfully sponsored the first national mine-safety legislation in 1968, after a cave-in at Farmington, West Virginia, killed scores of miners.

From the beginning, Hechler wanted to ban stripping outright and grant enforcement responsibility to the Environmental Protection Agency. After the Buffalo Creek disaster, the Nixon administration introduced a weaker bill that would have given states chief responsibility for regulation, overseen by the Bureau of Mines—then widely considered a political arm of the mining industry. Representative Morris Udall of Arizona engineered a compromise that included strong federal standards, allowed strip-mining under restricted conditions, and placed the law in the hands of the new Office of Surface Mining (OSM) in the Department of Interior.

Hechler opposed the compromise, warning his colleagues, "You know the economic and political history of this nation. You know the realities of economic and political pressure. You know that neither a state legislature nor any administrative authority can stand up against the wealth and power of a dominant economic group." Indeed, "King Coal" had long ruled state politics, with coal companies on the right and the equally imperial United Mine Workers of America on the left. Now, with mining jobs disappearing and retired miners dying, the UMWA has entered the late stages of a long fade. The coal industry, though, still owns half of the land in the Appalachian coalfields, and as much as 75 percent in West Virginia's top coal-producing counties. At the peak of the first stripping

boom in the early 1970s, a study found that every
governor and president of the state senate in the previous twenty years had worked in the coal industry
before taking office, afterward, or both. The current
governor, Cecil Underwood, who long worked in the
coal industry, received more than 20 percent of his
campaign contributions and 30 percent of the cost of
his million-dollar inauguration from coal.

Remaking the Law

Hechler had predicted that as long as the coal industry dominated Appalachia, an inch of regulatory lee-
way would rapidly become square miles of stripped
land. From the beginning, West Virginia's regula-
tions were peppered with omissions and innovative
interpretations. Newly hired field inspectors were
introduced to this "local version" of the law and in
some cases did their work unaware that they were
violating the law's actual requirements. When anti-
mining activists brought them to court and asked
them to read aloud the portions of the law that they
routinely violated, more than one state regulator
announced, "I've never seen that before."

Under a corrupt governor named Arch Moore,
who would later land in federal prison, coal companies went on a binge in the 1980s. They ignored basic
environmental standards while mining, ducked reclamation requirements by declaring bankruptcy, then
reconstituted themselves under different names and
went back to work. Investigative reporters, who did

much of the enforcement agency's job in this period, found multiple "companies" working in single underground mines and parent corporations spawning dozens of short-lived offspring.

West Virginia's environmental regulators have cleaned up their act considerably since then, but the DEP has maintained the habit of collaborating with the coal industry, producing a tangled map of discrepancies between state practices and the language and intent of federal law. Most dramatically, SMCRA requires that after stripping a company restore the disturbed land to its "approximate original contour"— that is, put it back more or less the way it was. According to the original federal act, companies can be exempted from this requirement only when the leveled land is put to a new, productive, and valuable "commercial or recreational" use. The thrust of the law is that mountaintop removal is an acceptable shortcut along the road to development that seems set to happen anyway, but that otherwise mountains should be left as they are.

Yet most mountaintop mining leaves landscapes undeveloped and isolated. State agencies in Virginia and Kentucky permit mountaintop removal for "wildlife and forest management," a category broad enough to catch any swath of land where trees might someday grow or deer browse. West Virginia counts a company's promise to open exhausted mining sites to hunters and fishermen as sufficient to make the land a "recreational facility." Neither approach is more than a dodge as long as hardwood forests refuse to grow on strip-mined land. Wildlife habitat is not improved by the elimination of forests and streams.

Enforcement has been as lax as the state's official policy is dubious. In 1997 and 1998 Ken Ward, a young reporter with *The Charleston Gazette*, West Virginia's largest-circulation newspaper, examined eighty-one permits for mountaintop-removal operations and found that sixty-one did not include even nominal exemptions from the approximate original contour requirement. That is, 75 percent of the operations were straightforwardly illegal.

Mountaintop removal probably violates several other clauses of federal law. SMCRA requires a comprehensive study of how strip-mining affects water systems, but no such study has ever been conducted. The federal Clean Water Act may bar the burial of streams with waste from mine sites, which would mean that valley fills are simply illegal. Moreover, while SMCRA requires that a company post sufficient insurance or collateral upon opening a mine to clean up the site afterward should it go bankrupt or simply abscond, lowball estimates and lax enforcement have left bond amounts well below what would be enough to clean up abandoned locations. The Office of Surface Mining estimates the deficit at $60 million. Others put it at ten times that amount.

All of this takes place under the oversight of the OSM. That agency's job is to ensure, through field inspections and annual reviews of state programs, that federal law is strictly enforced. The charge is demanding: SMCRA was an unusual piece of legislation, establishing elaborate requirements rather than broad guidelines for state programs, and making citation and punishment of any violation mandatory. These stipulations were an acknowledgment that corrupt collaboration between government and industry was the rule in the coalfields, and that only strong national standards could end that pattern.

The program began auspiciously. President Jimmy Carter's OSM hired administrators and field inspectors who were known for their commitment to enforcement. Inspectors shut down illegal mines and brought irresponsible operators to heel, over sometimes violent resistance. A few inspectors were taken hostage by entire crews of angry miners.

Then, after Ronald Reagan's election in 1980, things began to fall apart. Interior Secretary James Watt appointed OSM administrators who had previously worked to defeat SMCRA. They promptly approved state programs that, according to an OSM official who was with the agency then, "did not in any way, shape, or form meet the federal standards." For much of the 1980s, the agency was strained by low-level warfare between would-be enforcers and Reagan appointees, with the latter slowly gaining ground. The program reached its nadir under President George Bush's first OSM director, Harry Snider. Before exposure forced him from office, Snider made a practice of cutting private deals with companies to weaken enforcement, then imposing his arrangements in haranguing, wee-hour telephone calls to his underlings' homes.

Bill Clinton's 1992 victory raised hopes among the remnants of the original OSM staff, now a corps of toughened dissidents. Little had happened to meet those hopes by 1994, when Congress changed hands. The 1995 Republican Congress passed a 25 percent cut in the agency's program budget. The firings that followed fell heavily on field inspectors, in many cases the same ones who had spent years resisting Reagan-Bush administrators.

Since then, OSM inspections of mining sites have fallen by as much as 50 percent in some states. People within the OSM describe an isolated and nervous agency. Without active support from the Clinton administration, resented for its mere existence by industry, and scorned by disappointed environmentalists, the OSM is at constant risk of further cuts or complete elimination, and its agents tread carefully. Inspectors unhappily describe ignoring citizen complaints in communities where house foundations are cracked and water wells ruined by blasting. They know that the complaints are valid, but know also that they cannot uphold them without jeopardizing themselves or drawing fresh political attacks on the agency.

Coal's True Cost

This terrible history points the way to more basic questions. What are the long-term effects of removing mountaintops and filling valleys? Should mountaintop removal and other forms of strip-mining be legal? Should we rely as heavily as we do on coal?

No one knows what the legacy of mountain-top removal will be a century from now. Even the basic question of whether the valley fills will remain stable—a question inevitably posed in the shadow of the Buffalo Creek disaster—is uncertain. Some DEP employees declare complete confidence in the fills. Others are worried. A former OSM official who received a national award for his engineering work before leaving the agency says, "As time goes by, and these fills become saturated with water, they're going to begin to fail. I am convinced of that." Landslides have been reported at the feet of valley fills in Kentucky, but there is no consensus on whether those fills were typical or exceptionally ill-engineered.

Another unanswered question is how stripping will affect Appalachia's waterways. Life in rivers depends on the decaying leaves and other organic matter that small streams carry, which is reduced with every mile of valley fill. Moreover, no one knows the effects on drainage patterns and water tables of churning together complex layers of porous and non-porous rock.

Appalachia's water already carries a grim legacy of coal mining. Both strip-mining and traditional deep-mining disturb sulfur, which reacts with oxygen to produce acid water that can kill a stream. West Virginia's OSM branch estimates that two thousand miles of the state's rivers and creeks are "severely impacted" by acid runoff and other mine pollutants, and that many of those are dead. The OSM also acknowledges that as hundreds of mines in the state's high-sulfur coalfields close and the operators cease treating nearby water, thousands more miles will be endangered.

Coal is also the number-one culprit in generating acid rain, producing 70 percent of America's sulfur dioxide emissions and much greater amounts in places that still depend heavily on high-sulfur coal. The dead lakes of Russia and corroded statues of Eastern Europe begin with draglines and dynamite. Burning coal also releases twice as much carbon dioxide as natural gas and 50 percent more than oil and gasoline, making coal a leading cause of global warming. With the arguable exception of nuclear power, no other energy source displays such a dramatic gap between its price tag and its true cost.

The many kinds of harm that coal brings are all what economists call "externalities," costs or benefits that no one pays for directly. Mining and using coal is very costly—to landscapes, waterways, forests, the atmosphere—but no one who decides whether to mine coal, or to buy energy produced by coal, has to take that expense into account. The price of coal, in dollars, is the expense of getting it out of the ground and shipping it, plus a margin for companies' profits. The cost of getting coal out of the ground, in turn, is just the price of earthmoving equipment, dynamite, and wages. Companies keep strip-mining because it is cheap; people do not cut down their electric use, because power is cheap; and meanwhile the true costs of coal pile up around us but never come home as part of the economic decisions we actually make. There is a deep irresponsibility built into the country's energy economy, encouraging us to ignore the consequences of what we do in favor of the illusory efficiency of an energy boom that rests on ruination.

Things as They Are

Our destructive energy economy might be called a crisis of social ecology, a terrible distortion of the complex web of institutions and commitments in which our decisions are set. Considering the problem this way suggests a political response, which has recently become widespread among environmentally minded economists and economically minded environmentalists. They make an optimistic proposal, one that law can rework the social ecology into a more responsible form.

The main idea is that erasing coal's artificial cheapness is within the power of law. A favorite proposal is a "carbon tax" on fossil fuel emissions. This would mean taxing energy use in proportion to the amount of greenhouse gas that it produces. The price of gasoline would go up. Electricity produced by coal would go up more. The price of natural gas would increase, but by less. Together, these changes would alter everyone's day-to-day experience. Coal would no longer be the world's least expensive fuel, because its price would reflect some of its destructive effect. Mining companies would lose their unearned economic advantage. Power companies would have reason to use less-polluting energy sources, such as natural gas, rather than coal. Some might even look more seriously at solar and wind power, areas where technical progress has been promising but where research investment remains low.

If the carbon tax worked as imagined, individuals would have reason to make more responsible choices as well. High-mileage cars would offer meaningful savings. The industrial agriculture that depends on cheap, polluting fuel to keep its prices low might give way, sometimes, to locally grown, possibly organic products. Of course, ordinary people pay taxes, and energy taxes in particular would hit the poor and working people especially hard. Here too, though, the advocates of the carbon tax have an answer. For them, rearranging social ecology means making good decisions easier as bad decisions become less pleasant. Money gained from a carbon tax could pay for a reduction in the payroll tax, meaning that people would keep more of their paychecks and employers would pay less for each worker. If the economic models are right, this should mean more jobs and better pay. Some of the carbon-tax money could also fund tax breaks for research into environmentally friendly energy, encouraging industries to create jobs there rather than in less socially beneficial areas.

These are commendable ideas. Their intentions are good and, on the largest scale, their analysis is sound.

The destruction of Appalachia is a terrible symptom of a blinkered economic logic that needs changing. In the end, although we may save one beleaguered region instead of another, it is doubtful that we can save all or even most unless we first recast what I have been calling our social ecology.

Still, somehow, these ideas are not enough. They come easily to the tongue, yet they do not come easily into the world. Pronounced more than a few times, they begin to sound like cant. If we have been listening to public policy talk, or if we have been visited by the missionaries of total quality management or some other intellectual fad, we recognize in them a family resemblance to the jargon of the optimistic bureaucrat, the "win-win" designer, the consensus builder who, if he could just get enough of the best people into the same room, is sure he could bring everyone to see the one best solution. These good ideas display some of the same unreality that has infected public life at large.

In the course of his speech at Hobet 21, Bruce Babbitt called the ruined site "proof that we can have a vital economy and live in equilibrium with the landscape." For Babbitt, in that moment in West Virginia, words became a screen between the speaker and the world, concealing the shape and texture of things in the gauze of anodyne phrases. That kind of talk, almost everybody senses, does not appreciate the difficulties with which the world presents us. There are many things that, in good conscience, are difficult to oppose. Environmental conservation is one of them.

Prosperity, up to a point, is another, and so is efficient energy production. The higher the level of abstraction, the more of these good causes it is possible to support at once: the further a person is from any particular place, the less conflict he is likely to see among them. Babbitt was able to support all of them concurrently, without blinking. So do the advocates of that very good idea, the carbon tax. Such comprehensive advocacy excites suspicion, and rightly so. Unearned optimism ends by earning skepticism, or even by licensing despair. Earning hope, in contrast, requires a more severe gaze, one able to make hard distinctions between real and unreal prospects.

To my mind, one of the most powerful testaments to this idea comes not from Appalachia, but from my other touchstone region, Central Europe. It is *The Captive Mind*, by the Pole Czeslaw Milosz. Milosz won the Nobel Prize for literature in 1980 for his poetry, but he wrote this book at midcentury, just after leaving a position as a cultural attaché for the newly Communist Polish government and going into exile in the West. The book is a study of how Milosz's contemporaries, the writers and intellectuals of the anti-Nazi resistance, accommodated themselves to the coming of communism. Its core is a set of four biographical sketches, named by the first four letters of the Greek alphabet. Alpha is a writer of morality tales, stories in which people stand for principles, and succeed or fail as their principles do. A nominal Catholic and a conservative opponent of fascism, he becomes one of the pet writers of the new regime. He is drawn to communism because of its moral certainty and its celebration of the same common people that he has always lionized but never really understood. Communism's conceit that society and history are foremost a drama of competing principles, and that to understand that drama is to see the world clearly, fits his desire to see his vision and his prose reflected in the world. As a devotee of the idea of purity and a practitioner of its rhetoric, he becomes the deeply compromised spokesman of an increasingly corrupt regime.

Milosz calls Beta his "disappointed lover," the man whose passion for the world turns in the end to violent revulsion. Beta is a socialist, devoted to the idea of equality and harmony among people and nations. Desiring these is, for him, what it means to live. During the war he is imprisoned in the concentration camp at Dachau, where he sees men and women, guards and prisoners alike, turned into brutes and torturers. Emerging, he writes a scrupulous documentary of how the strong prisoners preyed on the weak, mothers rejected their faltering children rather than be shot with them, and clever men—including him—won the affection of the guards and survived the war as double agents. The book, though, does not purge his horror. Humanity, which he had loved above all, now appears bestial, "*naked* and ruled only by a few physiological principles." Repulsed by this terrible organism, he embraces Stalinism as the last hope of his old passion, a doctrine violent and relentless enough to purify the world and make it again able

to support his love. He becomes a vituperative ideo-
logue of the regime, living for each new chance to
attack what is frail, sick, and needy in the people he
cannot bear to call his fellows. Perhaps inevitably, he
ends by asphyxiating himself with gas.

The rest of Milosz's essays are equally unsettling.
His book may prove the most lasting indictment
of European communism. Yet when it was first
published, it was attacked from left and right alike.
Western Communists hated Milosz because he had
exposed the human sickness of the regime they sup-
ported. Conservatives and many liberals abhorred his
sympathy for the motives of his old friends, his sense
that communism was neither a brute force nor the
bureaucratization of evil, but for many a form of tor-
tured love. Milosz was incomprehensible to people
who had accepted the expectation of the time, that
intellectuals should line up on one or the other side of
the conflict between East and West, and anathematize
whatever came across the line.

This was, for Milosz, a version of his friends' failure to *see* the world as it was, to encounter individual
women and men as suffering and compromised, yet
somehow still alive with possibility. In documenting
this failure, his book posed an answer to it: the moral
necessity of "the passionate pursuit of the real," an
attention at once generous and severe toward one's
surroundings. He wrote social criticism as a poet,
unable by his vocation to let particular things be more
or less than they were. Any other attitude, he suggested, would amount to a betrayal of one's own

capacity for vision. Self-inflicted blindness, in turn, was the way to betraying the world. He had witnessed some of the century's great acts of treachery, and discerning how loyalty could still be possible was paramount for him. His answer lay in the strictures of attentiveness.

That same attentiveness is where we must begin to develop an honest view of our energy economy. Our natural-resource industries rest on the sacrifice of one region after another. The coalfields of Appalachia follow the copper mines of Montana, the pit mines for coal and gold in Wyoming and Colorado, and the clear-cuts of Washington, Oregon, and Alaska. Our hidden costs are hidden only as long as we avert our eyes from these places. The longer we continue, the less we can stand to view with a clear gaze. The cost of environmental destruction is real. We must only decide whether we will acknowledge it.

Law and Responsibility

Bringing attentiveness to law and policy is terribly important because they, like other public things, pervade our lives and affect the possibility of living responsibly. When we let public talk take on an air of unreality, we are letting ourselves ignore something whose importance we cannot escape. Neglecting reality only ensures that we will come on it unprepared.

Vaclav Havel's insistence that "we are all guilty" reminds Czechs that the regime of surveillance, coercion, and repression touched everyone at one time or another, and none reached 1989 untainted. In the same way, we are all caught up in our economy, with its legal boundary lines. So far as it is a destructive economy, we are destructive. So far as it is an exploitative economy—and much American industry, especially abroad, is exploitative, no matter what excuses are made for it—we are exploitative. There is no evading this in fact, although we are virtuosos at its emotional and intellectual evasion.

When public speech takes on reality, it is often in small and local ways. Cities across the country, including Boston, Los Angeles, and Minneapolis–St. Paul, have passed "living wage laws" requiring companies that contract with city government to offer health benefits and pay their workers enough to keep a family of four out of poverty. Living-wage laws adjust the logic of local economies in a modest fashion, changing the positions of a few thousand, perhaps as many as ten thousand people in a fair-sized city. Just as important, such laws are a palpable assertion of responsibility and an experiment in hope. Passing a living-wage law acknowledges that the economy is not a natural fact whose rules we have to accept, nor even a creature only of Congress, Wall Street, and the Federal Reserve. A living-wage law proposes that making a responsible economy, however imperfect and incomplete, can begin in palpable personal—and public—acts.

Those acts do something for the imagination. They divest of some of its unreality the platitude that the economy should be governed by principles of fairness.

It is easy enough to talk about international accords tying trade agreements to safe working conditions, decent pay, and education systems that prepare children for something more than sweatshop work. It is no more difficult to recall that there is no near-term prospect for such agreements, and that we can hardly conceive of the many practical problems they would present. The usual response to this ill-fitted pair of thoughts is to fall into a vaguely well-intentioned, or mildly guilty, assent to wherever one happens to be. Hope for a responsible economy depends on people's being committed to the idea of such an economy and finding ways to make their commitment effective. Again, except among the delusional, there can be no commitment to unreal things. Without work that makes the moral dimensions of the economy real for us, we will remain oblivious to them.

We need local work, then, and also national policies that make themselves felt in people's lives. However, although we most easily appreciate what we meet in person, we cannot afford to restrict our attention to that scale. Economies whose scope is national and international require governance with equal reach, and the imagination that is required to think seriously of such governance is not easily attained. It is an educated imagination, able not only to understand general principles through local efforts, but also to perceive local events as they are caught up in much larger schemes of production, exchange, and political and economic power. The idea of a carbon tax becomes a bit more real in the mind of someone who grasps the logic of the energy economy, who can understand how law, profit, and loss in their present arrangement enforce destructive practices. The energy economy has this in common with a good deal of what concerns law today: it is in equal measure central to our lives and distant from our thought and understanding. Closing that gap, by training our attention on the opaque, unwieldy, but pervasively influential laws and institutions that surround us is difficult but indispensable work. We have no other way to make real to the mind what already is all too real in the world, and so no other way to make it better.

These questions are real for us only so far as we are attentively and accurately aware of them. Considering strip-mining alongside general arguments about efficiency, or property rights, or the growth of the national economy should remind us that responsible thought must resist obscuring abstractions. Tocqueville noted that Americans in his day used abstract words more readily than concrete ones, and spoke as if "eventualities" were just as real as the worry that tearing down a mountain might release acid water into local streams. We risk making the same mistake every time we speak of "well-being" or "efficient energy production" without understanding that we are discussing whether or not to tear down mountains—not mountains in general, moreover, but the peaks of a few thousand square miles of central Appalachia, or the site of the battle of Blair Mountain. This abstraction is not morally honest: it permits us to believe that we are simply getting as much as possible of a good thing, when in fact we are choosing where and whom to sacrifice for it. Only when we understand that may we begin to take seriously the development of a law and economy that demand fewer sacrifices of communities and natural places.

No one who knew West Virginia and respected accurate speech could have spoken as Bruce Babbitt did at Hobet 21. Neither could anyone, just dropped from a helicopter, who managed to be attentive to his setting. The kind of attentiveness that Babbitt failed to achieve is indispensable to speech and thought that can make necessary distinctions and bear the weight of hope. Paying attention to Appalachia, like attending to any particular place, is a way of disciplining the obtuse, abstracting tendency he displayed. It reminds us that these matters are not easy, on any level. Yet we cannot complete good work in this realm without laws and policies, and so the need to understand these well is redoubled.

Attentiveness helps us to see what can and what cannot support our hope, and so it may be our best stay against despair. The temptation to despair of public things finds some encouragement in the story of mountaintop removal. However, the same terrible history also provides a reminder of how public hope becomes possible. Mountaintop removal has advanced merrily for more than twenty years. The new battle over it began when *The Charleston Gazette* let Ken Ward write regularly on mountaintop removal for more than a year, supporting him with editorials and op-ed essays against the practice. If mining laws are enforced in Appalachia, the enforcement will come about partly because of Ward's work, partly because dogged citizens' groups will continue to press state and federal agencies to turn law into fact. These citizens and the state's braver journalists have brought about nearly every moment of adequate environmental protection since 1980. They were also a good part of the force behind the passage of SMCRA in 1977. Without their investigative articles, lawsuits, and relentless monitoring, law and practice in environmental regulation would have split so far apart in West Virginia that the idea of the rule of law would be a regrettable joke, rather than a badly embattled principle.

Ward and his allies stand in a long line of Appalachians who, alongside their other work, have taken their stand against the depredations of coal. Lawyer Harry Caudill, the author of *Night Comes to the Cumberlands*, devoted his public career to recording the destruction of his native landscape. His writing had the truth of lifelong experience and the tension of an anger too deep to be overcome, which to be endured had to be turned to work. He titled another book, an account of strip-mining in contemporary Kentucky, *My Land Is Dying*. That heart-cry echoed through everything he wrote. Wendell Berry has given his adult life to documenting the competing principles of preservation and exploitation in his home state of Kentucky. None of these is a narrowly political figure, but all are eminently public. Without them, public things would fail.

Law depends on both a culture of enforcement among those charged with implementing it, and participation by the citizens who are nominally responsible for making it and inescapably charged with living under it. Mining law has been distorted in Appalachia by the failure of the first. It has been incompletely saved by the vitality of the second. Only when some number of people are committed to treating the law as a public affair, as a task of maintaining the commons, can law fill that role. Indeed, only then can we credibly think of it as having that role. Without that kind of thought the commons will suffer, and so will we who depend on them.

In turn, if law is to do some of the work that we most need, then the same work must also take place outside of law, in our own lives. Law is intimately related to our practices of responsibility and irresponsibility, yet there is a terrible air of unreality in proposals for legal "fixes" such as the carbon tax. These policies encounter an obdurate fact: we do not live in a way that either invites or promises to uphold a "responsible economy" that is merely legislated. We sense, although we do not welcome the perception, that too much talk of wise policy is premised on the pretense that we can become responsible without changing ourselves, just by changing the prices of things.

In such basic matters, reform through law is

effective only if it joins with lives that realize some of the principles that law declares and tries to enforce. If we do not become the sort of people—more reflective in our demands, more modest in our needs, more attentive in our action—who could inhabit a responsible economy, such an economy will not come to us by law or government. Because it will not come without law and government, changing ourselves is all the more important. We are the beginning as well as the end of a decent economy's possibility, because we are the sole site of responsibility. Responsibility begins in attentiveness, because only that can help us to discern the conditions of hope.

CHAPTER FIVE

The Neighbor and the Machine: Technology and Responsibility

There is a law of neighbourhood which does not leave a man a perfect master on his own ground.

—Edmund Burke

THE MEANING of words changes when the reality that they describe falls away from under them, or takes a new, unrecognizable shape. Changes in the meaning of words draw a kind of map, in language, of changes in the world.

Take the word *neighbor*. Traditionally, anywhere in this country, people who lived in the same place knew and accommodated one another by necessity. When most people worked the land, as was true in this country just a century ago, neighbors relied on some of the same fields, streams, and ponds in caring for their livestock. Anyone had the power to ruin one of these common resources, and everyone understood what a terrible act that would be. At a minimum, any two neighbors relied on a common fence that both, by mutual understanding, shared in maintaining. Although few formal ties constrained them, each knew that the other could be relied on to do his share in replacing torn wire or fallen stones, or recovering a strayed cow. Neglecting these tasks was a serious failing, enough to put a man outside his neighbors' society.

Because they necessarily shared work, neighbors knew one another. When only handwritten letters, newspapers, and books connected them regularly with the world beyond their home village or valley, they generally knew one another as more than work-mates. At church, political events, dances, and other gatherings, their personalities wore into one another, producing eccentric patterns of tolerance, accommodation, and affection. A neighbor was as much a part of the character of a place as the shape of the land or the quality of local government, and often more than the latter.

I do not mean to be pious or nostalgic toward this old practice of neighborliness. It is important to understand, though, how much nearness once meant for people's relations to one another. Its importance has been fading for more than a hundred years. It was that fading, and not a living tradition, that Robert Frost documented in "Mending Wall," in which he meets his neighbor for the springtime ritual of replacing the stones that winter frost-heave has loosened from the wall that follows the border of their half-abandoned farms. Frost calls the affair "just another kind of outdoor game, / One on a side. It comes to little more: There where it is we do not need the wall: / He is all pine and I am apple orchard. / My apple trees will never get across / And eat the cones under his pines, I tell him." When Frost points this out, his neighbor answers, "Good fences make good neighbors," and Frost reflects, "*Why* do they make good neighbors? Isn't it / Where there are cows? But here there are no cows."

At the poem's end, Frost imagines his neighbor a primeval savage who "will not go behind his father's saying," the adage about good fences making good neighbors, to find its purpose and see whether it still holds—whether the maxim retains its force or is obsolete. The answer is that a landscape without cows, an unworked landscape, no longer requires the old disciplines. Instead it invites Frost's individualist whimsy, "something that does not love a wall, / That wants it down." Frost knows, and his neighbor does not, that the whole practice of neighborliness is disappearing, as it were, between their chapped hands. Our fathers' sayings can remain ours only if "behind" them is material reality, a way of spending our hours and energies that gives them life.

Today, the latest use of *neighbor* is on the Internet. "Neighbors" are people deemed to have similar tastes by the programs that on-line booksellers and music merchants use to recommend new titles to their regular customers. The programs draw on previous purchases to project future interests. In a curious way, the new use is exactly right: neighbors are connected by commonalities in how they pass their time, what they worry about, what they are likely to exult over. The rightness, though, is obscured by the hollowing-out that neighborliness has undergone in a century in which proximity has become less a shared predicament than a bare fact. The neighbor happens to live next door, but nothing in the way he makes his living, entertains himself, or pursues friendship and romance has anything more to do with us than with anyone else in the same town, or in the next state, or on the other coast. The walls are all down.

This is the sort of change that worried Thoreau when he wrote, "We do not ride on the railroad; it rides upon us." A thousand small changes in our lives will in turn change the communities, even the cultures, in which we live. They will rob words of their meaning, which is to say, take from us ways of thinking about ourselves and the world, and they will give words new meanings that would once have been inconceivable. The most powerful of these changes now occur in technology, from Thoreau's railroad, which connected farms, towns, and cities, and heralded the automobile that eliminated the old idea of neighborliness, to the information systems that have given the old notion a new, disembodied life.

Just as every decision in law and politics is a choice about what we are to become, so every new use of technology in some measure heralds our next form. If we enter into these changes heedlessly, as if their sum were as minor as each seems in its moment, we risk becoming inadvertently unrecognizable to ourselves, murmuring with T. S. Eliot's Prufrock, "That is not what I meant at all." It is urgently important that we practice responsible thinking about technology.

Thinking of Genes

Genetic engineering exemplifies the need to think through technology. It elicits an ambivalence that pervades our responses to technological change. Optimistically, it permits us to imagine preventing congenital disorders such as Down's syndrome, developing new treatments for diabetes and other illnesses, and even changing our genes to make our lives longer and healthier than ever in the past. Yet some products of the new technology strike us as wrong, or at least deeply unsettling. Scientists have developed techniques for producing frogs with no heads or central nervous systems, inevitably conjuring images of mindless "human beings" harnessed as organ farms. Princeton University molecular biologist Lee Silver predicts that, within a few centuries, genetic engineering will have made us into a multiclass society, where the GenRich (genetically rich) do all the important and remunerative work while the Naturals (people like us) sweep floors and care for other people's children.

Genetic technology expresses a basic truth about technological change, and puts it in terms stark enough to capture and hold our attention. The prospect of widespread genetic engineering makes explicit what we have tended to leave implicit, or to acknowledge uncomfortably and in passing: in making new technology we remake ourselves.

If we are to take the assessment of technology at all seriously, we must be able to evaluate such a radical phenomenon as biotechnology. This means considering how our prospective new powers might affect our capacity to uphold certain of our defining values. This is not a matter of social forecasting so much as it is a reflection of moral sensibility. We know something of our best and worst possibilities, and have some idea of how the best are maintained and where the worst are engaged. How does a new technology promise to interact with these, and where might it take them?

Viewed through these questions, the ambivalence we feel on first encountering genetic technology comes into sharper focus. As a first try, we might put the problem this way. Genetic engineering promises to advance the core modern values of humanitarianism—the commitment to pressing back the boundaries of death and suffering—and free self-development toward personal fulfillment and excellence. At the same time, though, the new technology threatens to undermine the equally important commitment to equality, as both a social goal and a moral view about the bedrock importance of human beings. That change would have grave consequences for morality and public life. Grasping this possibility, and seeing its relation to the myriad benefits that accompany it, is the essential work in assessing the new biology.

For all the excitement that genetic engineering has generated, no scientist has changed the heritable genetic makeup of a human being. The "genetic therapies" in use or in development are mainly super-medicines; for example, bacteria are engineered to produce insulin, then injected into a diabetic's body, where they do the work that her own cells cannot. Similarly, cystic fibrosis patients inhale a solution of cold virus with an admixture of the genetic material that produces healthy lung functions. If the patient catches the cold, his lung cells may take up some of the healthy material, and so work normally for a period.

However, public debate has concentrated on techniques that change genes heritably, introducing something new into the line of descent. Such engineering remains hit-and-miss, but has become commonplace in laboratory animals. Its products include lines of mice that contain human genetic material, and farm animals that have been engineered to produce medically valuable substances, usually in their milk. There is no reason to think that the comparative modesty of the current technology will last long. Most experts anticipate a radical increase in the sophistication and reliability of engineering techniques. Meanwhile, the Human Genome Project, a well-funded effort to map the 100,000 human genes, is optimistically expected to produce a complete picture by 2005. Although not everyone agrees with Lee Silver's view that thoroughly engineered "designer babies" will become possible by the middle of the next century, no one denies that our trajectory is taking us that way, with no expectation of a sudden stop.

As the technology develops, scientists, ethicists, and activists have weighed in with proposed lines between acceptable and unacceptable procedures. The hardest line going, already a rearguard affair, holds that people have no business tampering with genes, ever. This opinion has meaningful support in many religious communities, and a joint statement several years back by a variety of religious leaders condemned the prospect of scientists' patenting new forms of life.

This view rests on the idea that some realms of the natural order should stay off limits to human activity. However, this principle tends to lose its appeal when it is applied to particular cases. Not many people would be willing to deny genetically enhanced treatment to a diabetic or a cystic fibrosis patient on the grounds that these techniques are less natural than any number of synthetic drugs and chemical therapies that we use every day. If we could cure Tay-Sachs disease at birth, refusing to do so would be outrageously cruel; denying a prenatal cure for the same disease because of a distinction between the genes and the rest of the body has the same terrible ring. We believe strongly in reducing suffering, and doing so through genetically engineered bacteria strikes most of us, on reflection, as continuous with the ways that we currently work to achieve this.

Most proposed limits on genetic engineering acknowledge the power of the humanitarian impulse, and try to draw a line between cure and "enhancement." Once the line is clear, cures are permitted and enhancement is forbidden. This has long been a prominent proposal among professional bioethicists, and has made many more appearances in professional journals than in the popular press. It has received relatively little popular attention mostly because, as even professional ethicists have begun to acknowledge, it doesn't work. The line won't stand still.

This is true partly because of problems of definition. There is no single human baseline of "health." We exercise, take vitamins, and eat well not to "enhance" ourselves beyond simple health, but to "be healthy." So, in a certain way, "enhancement" is a part of "health." At the same time, for anyone with a congenital defect, being genetically adjusted to an average level of functioning *is* plainly an enhancement, and as such is not different in kind from going all the way up to the maximum, "healthiest" level.

These are technical reasons for the shifting line. There are cultural reasons as well, and the two interact powerfully. Contemporary culture, particularly in a line of thought rooted in Wilhelm von Humboldt and John Stuart Mill, is deeply committed to the idea that people should be able to develop their talents as fully as possible and acquire new ones if they can. This is now a large part of what we mean by "liberty." We accept that parents should be able to send their children to good schools, that those who can afford the cost may hire personal trainers, and that people who learn languages or take up instruments are behaving well, even commendably. One of the most common defenses of the free market, in the time that it faced real competition from authoritarian socialism, was that markets allow individuals to pursue—if not always attain—the careers that they find most fulfilling. All of this leaves us reluctant to honor a dividing line when, just on the other side, we glimpse a richer life. So we are reluctant to draw a line and stay on one side of it.

Acknowledging both of these difficulties suggests that some enhancement—whatever we mean by that—is inevitable. Some people devote a good deal of hopeful speculation to the topic. Philip Kitcher, a philosopher of science, proposes in *The Lives to Come* a "utopian eugenics" in which parents will select their children's attributes as they see fit. Although he envisages no legal restrictions on these selections, Kitcher assures his readers that families will participate in "widespread public discussion of values and the social context of decisions" and be guided by "universally shared respect for difference coupled with a public commitment to realizing the potential of all who are born." Thanks to this commitment, Kitcher writes, a just system of universal health care will make the same genetic procedures available to all families.

Kitcher believes that the liberal commitment to humanitarianism and equality can coexist happily with genetic libertarianism. In assessing this optimism, it is instructive to consider the picture of utopian eugenics that Lee Silver presents in *Remaking*

Eden: Cloning and Beyond in a Brave New World. Silver merrily spins out a libertarian tale of biotechnology's future that is untrammeled by Kitcher's liberal niceties. Silver predicts that "the power to change the nature of humankind" will lead to exponential growth in differences between the engineered GenRich and the Naturals. Presenting an imagined history of the next millennium, he writes, "[In 2350] [a]ll members of Congress, all entrepreneurs, all other professionals, all athletes, all artists, and all entertainers were members of the GenRich class." Then, engineering begins to multiply varieties of GenRich populations: "By the middle of the twenty-seventh century, there were at least a dozen different species of human descendants having chromosome numbers that varied from forty-six in Naturals to fifty-four in the most enhanced GenRich individuals."

The point of Silver's proposals is not their plausibility. Predicting complex and distant innovations is impossible in principle, because we cannot know whether they would work without a detailed picture of *how* they would work—and anyone who had such a picture would in effect have brought about the predicted innovation. Silver's technological forecasting is particularly suspect, since the workings of genetics remain largely mysterious, and no one can say with confidence what kinds of technological innovation should in principle be possible, let alone which ones will come to pass. Long-range scientific speculation belongs to science fiction, and here perhaps to science fantasy.

However, fantasy reveals a good deal about those who cultivate it. Knowing as little as we do about genetics, we almost inevitably use debates over genetic engineering as sounding boards for our social, political, and ethical aspirations and fears. Our ways of thinking about technology find unconstrained expression in this murky yet wide-open field. Seen in this light, Silver's extremism exemplifies two moral dangers. His attitude to technology amounts, in the terms of Thoreau's metaphor, to lying across newly laid railroad tracks in eager anticipation of the oncoming train. Silver's enthusiasm is almost a kind of vitalism, a celebration of the power of nature, technology, and human ingenuity to destroy old forms of life and give rise to new ones. This attitude attends much less to the relative worth of what is destroyed and what created than to the heady process of creative destruction itself.

One is properly reminded here of the impresarios of *Wired* magazine. In his book *Out of Control*, editor Kevin Kelly proposes that the old line between "the born and the made" has become irretrievably blurred. Biotechnology, especially genetic engineering, has begun to insert technical achievements into organisms. At the same time, self-replicating computer programs that mimic evolutionary processes by developing unplanned order, as well as the early stages of "artificial intelligence," bring the dynamics of living things into machinery.

According to Kelly, technological changes enable us to see what has always been true but hitherto hidden. Life consists not of carbon-based organisms, but of any self-ordering, self-reproducing system of phenomena—what Kelly calls a "vivisystem." We are vivisystems, but so too are computer systems, market economies, and "hybrid patches of nerve and silicon." Moreover, Kelly speculates, life has a tendency to spread itself into previously inert matter, fighting back against entropy and slowing the death of the universe. By passing from us into computers, "Life has conquered carbon" and moved on, leaving humanity "a mere passing station on hyperlife's gallop into space."

All of this might seem to be the froth of an overexcited, idiosyncratic mind, and in part it is. However, Kelly carries to its revealing extreme a widespread attitude to technology that he shares with Silver. Take the economic dislocation that follows the transition from industrial to information economies. In 1997, Kelly wrote in *Wired*, "In a poetic sense, the prime task of the Network Economy is to destroy— company by company, industry by industry—the industrial economy." The idea that we might have an obligation at least to ease the change so that the new economy does not leave many wrecked lives in its wake is alien to his point of view. Knowing that Kelly considers economic transition an evolutionary triumph of one vivisystem over another, in which people are only "a way-station," illuminates the rhapsodic tone of his description.

In the same vein, Kelly's techno-romanticism guides *Wired* to scorn ecological concerns. Last year, UCLA biophysicist Gregory Stock, who "believes that

genetic engineering is the next stage in natural evolu-
tion," told the magazine: "The planet is undergoing a
massive extinction . . . we're at the center of it." We
shouldn't be concerned, though, because "modern
technology is a major evolutionary transition. . . . It
would be astonishing if that occurred without dis-
rupting existing life." To be sure, global warming and
the erosion of the ozone layer can be considered "evolutionary transitions," triumphs of the human and
industrial vivisystems, if one interprets the matter
insistently enough. Still, the reader is right to think
that something—perhaps the most important thing—
is lost in this interpretation. Kelly's biological ideas
underlie a giddy complacency toward any notion of
stewarding the natural world.

This complacency is intrinsic to the attitude that
Kelly and Silver share. When any transformation is
the fruit of life's battle against entropy, debating social
and economic change appears fatuous. Trends take on
an air of inevitability, and of inevitable goodness. Any
doctrine that celebrates the raw power of natural
processes as they flow through society will end by sac-
rificing the labor of responsible thought for the pleasures of vitalist enthusiasm. Kelly simply reaches the
conclusion more rapidly than most.

Silver inadvertently expresses the defining moral
danger of genetic engineering. He describes a world
in which humanity, as a condition that we have in
common, has disappeared. In this world, to call us
"equal" would seem almost a conceptual confusion.
Equality is distinct from sameness, to be sure, but

it does suppose enough commonality that the same projects, fears, and aspirations can make sense to everyone, and that all face at least commensurable limitations and hazards. What care we take for other people, especially but by no means only those outside our immediate circles of love, is caught up with a sense that we share a common vulnerability. We are affected by the recognition that suffering, physical and psychic, is unavoidable, that loneliness is ineradicable, and that our lives all go downward to the same death. At our best we are affected by what Jan Patocka, a Czech philosopher and dissident who died after a beating by the Czechoslovak secret police, used to call "the solidarity of the shaken": the cleaving together of those who recognize how easily they can be riven apart from one another, from what they value most, and even from their lives. This is a defense and maintenance of the human world that emerges from the recognition of that world's fragility.

Some of the ambitions that biotechnology taps, and the fantasies that it ignites, threaten just this sense of common value and common endangerment. Excusing some individuals and even some classes from imperfection, mediocrity, and vulnerability to many sorts of physical suffering invites opting out of concern for the less bountifully endowed. It aspires to remove what, in Frost's word, is "behind" the concern for one another that is so much of the substance of what we style moral equality. Laying new stone may transform some of us from the shaken to the unshakable, and leave others to shiver as they may.

This danger pervades biotechnology. It tempts us to deny responsibility. That should be the ultimate focus of our thought about technology in general. We need to discern where and how change might fray our sense of common humanity and stanch the sources of our moral concern.

To *the* Summum Malum

When our bedrock moral importance is eroded, the significance of our suffering also fades, and humanitarian values are threatened. Close to home, prenatal tests can already reveal susceptibility to a large and growing number of genetic disorders. Insurance companies are considering refusing coverage for illnesses that could have been predicted by testing, and parents who can afford the tests face the decision of whether to bring an "imperfect" child into the world. In the likely event that elaborate genetic screening—which is almost certain to be expensive for a great while, if not always—is more readily available to the affluent than to others, most congenital disorders will become "poor people's diseases." This is a damning designation for research funding, policy attention, and public concern.

Alongside the problem of equality is a broader humanitarian concern. If the choice to abort "defective" fetuses becomes more common, we should wonder whether these distinctions will shade over into other areas. What resources we commit to the congenitally disabled partly reflect a sense that their conditions are uncontrollable tragedies, which we are willing to share the burden of making less painful. However, just as we can be made kind or humble by inevitable things, so we are impatient and sometimes cruel toward imperfection that we believe to be avoidable. The more we can select against these inconvenient fellow citizens, the more likely we are to grow callous in our treatment of them. When the question "What right do you have to exist" actually has some sense, the conclusion "Your life is no business of mine" takes on a grim plausibility.

Genetic enhancement poses more severe risks. It may be that we are within a half-century of enabling affluent parents to select the best-endowed of many fertilized embryos, and even of inserting genes for the highest physical, musical, or intellectual potential into otherwise unremarkable DNA codes. Although it is not yet possible to confirm or disprove Silver's speculation, there is no good reason for confidence that it will not eventually be possible to add radically enhanced or wholly new capacities.

The more modest vision is worrisome enough. In effect, well-to-do parents could make the myth of aristocratic excellence a reality by ensuring the potential excellence of their children. Over a few generations, our class divides could be written into our genes, with the excellent retaining their prominence generation after generation. In this setting, there would be great temptation to abandon the goal of social equality in favor of a "rational" sorting out of tasks according to innate gifts. And, of course, as social division became deeper and more blithely accepted, mutual moral indifference would seem ever more natural.

Even the more modest scenarios bode ill for democracy and humane practices. The great liberal John Stuart Mill believed that the votes of the educated should count more than those of the lower classes, and that "primitive" peoples like those of India were unworthy of self-government. Deep and ineradicable differences among persons would invite a renewal, not necessarily of those institutional distinctions, but of the spirit that deeply discounts certain groups' contributions to democratic debate. Moreover, inequality and fading moral concern can only weaken institutions designed to help the weakest and least fortunate. In both cases, we are talking not about a new problem, but about a new exacerbation of existing problems.

Other reasons for worry have to do with subtle features of moral temperament. Central to our honoring others' moral importance is the acknowledgment that their lives unfold by designs that we cannot make for them, or alter beyond a modest measure. Yet we contemplate a world where parents' anticipated delight in a child might have less to do with the mysterious grace of reproduction than with the assurance that they have selected the embryo that can replicate its mother's career as a concert pianist, or be the football star its father never was—or just be lovable because it is "perfect."

Considering this possibility highlights a confusion between two ways that we love. We love the things that we have made, mainly, because they are as we planned them, envisioned them, wanted them. If we make them successfully, they are perfect in that word's original sense: made all the way through, finished according to design. We love them as the consummation of our will and imagination in the world. They present our wishes and work, tangible before us, complete.

The way that we aspire to love people is very different. We are all imperfect—never done—and are the products of no person's will or design. At our best, we love others not because they reflect our desires and designs, but that they offer us what we could not have made, or perhaps even imagined. They are beyond us, independent of us, and yet, sometimes, they come to us of their own accord. What parents love in children—either at first or after hard learning—is not what they have made, but what they have participated in bringing into being. They have helped to create something bound to seek independence from them, but capable of freely loving them.

By inviting this confusion, biotechnology has the power to foster the worst kind of indifference. The conviction that our own desires are the world's compass points is among the greatest barriers to genuine respect for other individuals. The more able we become to treat others as vehicles for our own aims, the less readily we conceive of them as intrinsically important.

Mary Shelley's *Frankenstein*, a curiously relevant

story today, describes a man who creates life but cannot make it human. Frankenstein's monster is a sad, desperate, and eventually cruel creature because it cannot enter the world of mutual regard and care. The point of the book is how easily our power can outrun our capacity for responsibility. The question that it poses metaphorically we must now take literally: whether we can make humane the lives we make. As we accelerate the pace of technological change that in turn changes our lives and communities, the lives we make are our own.

Alongside its benefits, then, biotechnology plays dangerously into our impulse to treat others as vehicles for our desires, to be assessed by their convenience. It promises to deepen our inequalities and to make them more explicit and inescapable. In these ways, it promises to accelerate the trends of a time whose characteristic excesses are mutual indifference and the seductive illusion of self-reliance. Biotechnology could accelerate our self-fulfillment terrifically, but at severe cost to humanitarianism and equality. Most people are properly unprepared to sacrifice any of these commitments wholesale.

If this picture is accurate, then we should be looking not so much for a "line," a single, neat formula, as for the clearest possible view of how any new power affects the intricate balance among our basic values. It is fitting that that view should be powered partly by grim example—the *summum malum* of Silver's blithely presented dystopia, and the many minor horrors that might incline us toward it in the nearer term. Knowing the greatest danger that genetic engineering presents is one way to discerning clearly the good it might also bring.

Thinking Through Technology

It is with this in mind that I have discussed an issue that has already been tiresomely argued in many places. The promise of the biotechnology debates lies in their powerful concentration of the question of what technology means for our lives together. The prospect of genetic engineering has *made* technology a problem again, rather than an unquestioned force moving as irresistibly as nature itself—the reckless attitude of Lee Silver and *Wired*.

Our task is to turn a problem into a set of orienting questions, and some partial answers. I have been trying to show that this is possible in the vexed matter of biotechnology. My hope is that attention and intelligence will show its possibility in other areas as well.

This is now more important than ever. When we increase our control over the natural world, the resulting benefits always bring new dangers and responsibility. We bring another field of activity in from the background that sustains us while requiring little thought—the realm of our fathers' sayings—and rework it in ways that we do not always anticipate and sometimes cannot contain. From agricultural technology that massively increases yields but exhausts soil and pollutes groundwater to control over the fossil fuels that drive the modern economy but threaten to change the global climate irreversibly, we have had difficulty separating unprecedented gains from irremediable harm. In every case we have made the natural world and, indirectly, ourselves the objects of our own power. Now we take ourselves in hand, as it were, without mediation. More than ever, maintaining or altering nature and what can only be called the human condition is directly the responsibility of human intelligence and skill.

As this responsibility grows, our inclination to accept it does not increase proportionately. We are, by and large, attuned to what Garrett Hardin calls "intrinsic responsibility," the kind we experience when a thrown rock shatters a window or a poorly steered car slams into a guardrail. We expect the consequences of our acts to be straightforward and immediate. Yet the most severe harm we do today is very different from this. It is the result of the complex relationships between our energy consumption and strip-mining, or between the technology we accept for our own use and the sort of world that our descendants will inhabit. We are unaccustomed to thinking in this way, yet no other style of thought is adequate to the scope of our power to do damage.

There are several ways of responding to this difficulty. We can draw the lines of our activity as closely as possible, using technologies whose effects we can account for; we can eat food and use goods whose production we can trace in the same way. This is hardly simple, though, for even a kiwifruit, consumed in Boston, involves one in a web of technological effects that would have been impossible two centuries ago, from artificial fertilizers and pesticides to the diesel-fueled ship that carried the produce across a hemisphere and the air-conditioning that cools the supermarket where it is sold.

We can also attempt to reform our laws and our economy so that everyone's lines are drawn more closely, or at least more palpably. To take a simple example, imagine an environmental impact label, like a nutrition statement, on the package of every product in a store. The label might include an estimate of all fuels consumed, all poisons used, and all natural resources employed in the manufacture of the product, as well as a description of its byproducts and their disposal. To aid the imagination, the label might identify the processes, such as global warming, the depletion of the ozone layer, or the development of acid rain, to which the product contributed. A carbon tax would convey some of the same information, less articulately but perhaps even more effectively.

Whatever hope we find in such measures, though, it is doubtful that we can contend with technological change unless we develop an idea of relinquishment. It is a motto of some men and women who value their work, especially craftspeople, that we should make nothing we would not be remembered by. Today that creed needs completing with another principle: we should take, destroy, or change nothing in whose continuance we would wish our memory eventually to dissolve. Against the idea of an unyielding monument to our achievements, there stands the notion that our best achievement might be what we have let live for its own sake, and for love of the thought that it will outlast us by longer than we can imagine. After centuries of identifying triumph with the development of technology, from the steam engine to the lunar module, our greatest challenge now is the decision not to do what it is in our power to do. We will have to do so against our present convenience, for those to whom our comfort could deed great and uncompensated unhappiness. We will have to do so for common reasons.

We devote considerable energy to ascertaining the economic, environmental, and demographic consequences of our policies and technologies. These are important enterprises. But if we are to have what we might call wisdom, we must also ask what our practices are likely to make of us, and whether that prospect is compatible with what we think it fitting for us to be. It may be that our best ideals will flourish only if, alongside sound policies, women and men consciously surrender certain aspirations to self-remaking and accept the pleasures and limits of their humanity. Until now, in elemental ways we have simply been natural. Henceforth, to stay humane, we may have to conclude that we are all Naturals, and are better for it.

CHAPTER SIX

Irony and Ecstasy

I think that we may safely trust a good deal more than
we do. We may waive just so much care of ourselves
as we honestly bestow elsewhere.

—*Henry David Thoreau,* Walden

THIS BOOK is a plea for continued attention to
things that we have been neglecting. It is an argument that they remain necessary, and that neglecting
them is unwise and hazardous. Their neglect today
takes several forms. Often it begins in ironic avoidance of the world, the studied refusal to trust or hope
openly. Elsewhere it comes from reckless credulity, the
embrace of a tissue of illusions bound together by
untested hope. Sometimes neglect takes reassurance
from the Free Agent's conviction that life's best things
can be had in solitude.

One answer to this neglect is a renewed idea of
public responsibility, the active preservation of things
that we must hold in common or, eventually, lose altogether. This idea responds to the widespread perception that public life, especially politics, has ceased to

matter, that it only elevates bad characters and diminishes already small souls. It is an argument about the good that public activity offers the world and makes possible in a person's own life.

This idea of responsibility does not have the extraordinary qualities of much of this century's political activity. It does not resolve the questions of what sort of life is best to lead, or what kind of activity is right to undertake. Nor is it redemptive: it does not promise to make good every sacrifice and restore each loss by drawing up a small life into the vortex of social transformation, making it a sacrifice of imperfection to the achievement of perfection. It moves within, and not against, the human predicament.

The heart of this idea is that no response to our predicament is adequate, mature, or tenable if it does not attend to public responsibility. We take our stance toward public life in the way our work, relationships, and general way of living affect the commons. The commons are the things we all rely upon that can be preserved only by attention running beyond narrow self-interest. I have been writing about several sorts of commons, which affect us in different ways and require different sorts of maintenance. It is credible, I think, to conceive of them as a set of three interrelated ecologies. One is an interpersonal, moral ecology. In it are all the practices of generosity, thoughtfulness, commitment, and diligence that people convey to one another in family, friendship, and love. It moves by the gift of the trustworthy and well-tested personal example. Its failure is marked by the rise of selfishness, thoughtlessness, and indifference to obligation and effort. It moves through parents who manage to make gentle, prudent behavior expected rather than aberrant; through friends whose principled risks make courage credible; through teachers whose intellectual strictures are a part of their character, which they pass on to their students.

Starting from this idea helps us to think of public acts in terms not of where they take place, the old distinction between public and private, but rather as a matter of purpose and effect: public acts aim at maintaining the commons intelligently enough to have effect. Raising a child can be a public task, not in the sense of being governed by some political principle from outside the family, but because the parents understand the importance and fragility of what they are working to convey. A journalist who holds the powerful to hard standards of truth performs a public act. She helps to uphold a tenuous fit between political speech and political action, and stays the slide of public institutions toward corruption and contemptibility. So do people who devote themselves to environmental conservation, human rights, community organizing, or credibly motivated electoral politics.

All such work contributes to the second kind of commons, a broad social ecology. This commons includes the institutions and practices that affect the shape of our lives. These are our only means of deciding whether to control certain kinds of genetic engineering, or whether to continue energy policies that

ensure the destruction of central Appalachia's mountains. Besides yielding good or bad decisions for the
future, they provide our only way of safeguarding old
gains, from civil liberties to workers' right to orga-
nize, that erode when untended. The decisions that set
us in one direction or another are inescapable. Our
choice is whether to participate in making them, or to
let them be made by the concatenation of private
desire and public indifference.

The people who spend large portions of their lives
working in these realms are among the best of us; but
the importance of the social commons is great enough
that we should not leave their upkeep to these people
alone. They should be the further outcroppings of
a whole body of practical, public commitment, in
which everyone ought to have a share. Public work is
best considered not as a career, a view that tends to
excuse those who settle on other callings, but as an
aspiration that inflects all our decisions, about the
careers we choose and about the *way* we conduct our
careers and our lives.

The best way to understand this second commons,
of politics and civic life, is to reverse the idea that politics is the fulcrum on which all society, even all human
experience, can be radically changed. The disappointment of that idea is a source of our despairing irony,
and especially of our failure to find a satisfying way of
thinking and talking about politics. Discarding that
idea would mean returning to an older one: that politics is a portion of the public things on which we all
rely, and which we neglect only at the cost of avoiding

the world. Although not our supreme fulcrum, politics is the site of many of the decisions that draw us toward the preservation or the destruction of the commons.

The third sort of commons is ecology in its usual sense, the natural world to which we all, however uncertainly and ignorantly, trace our very lives. The preservation or neglect of the natural environment cannot be separated from the health of our political institutions. Neither, in turn, is at all independent of the condition of our personal practices. The several commons belong to one another. Responsibility toward them urges that we live our personal lives with an eye to the maintenance of public concerns, and in a way that permits us to move beyond ourselves and back again, drawing sustenance from a whole life in order to expend some of it in the necessary work of common things.

In the early 1970s, when the novelist Ken Kesey had returned to his hometown of Eugene, Oregon, to raise his children, write, and farm a bit, he was interviewed by a radical young journalist. The young man asked in concern, "Ken, why aren't you political anymore?" Kesey replied with perfect aplomb, "What do you mean, not political? I'm running for the school board."

The image of Kesey's running for the school board is especially poignant for me. School boards are not much admired these days. They are perceived at best as anachronistic, slightly silly institutions, less quaint than town meetings but no more relevant to an age of professional administration. More probably, in images of the Christian Coalition's grassroots electoral activism, they are launching pads for hacks and political extremists.

I have never been able to take this view of school boards, because they were the first site of public responsibility that I knew. When my mother was a school-board member, working to improve the beleaguered public schools of my home county, she was drawn into a statewide battle over the consolidation of rural elementary schools. The state government, enchanted by a crude notion of efficiency, had drawn up a list of "economies of scale"—minimum populations for each grade level in state schools. The standards, which might have been appropriate to a suburban district, had little to do with the reality of a rugged, thinly populated state. At the same time, West Virginia began a massive school-building program, funneling money into nearly every one of its fifty-five counties for new schools—which were funded, however, only if they met the economies of scale standards. Scores of schools in the small, far-flung communities that cover much of West Virginia were closed to form large, consolidated centers. Tens of thousands of elementary students now spend two to three hours each day traveling to and from these new, giant schools. The small communities whose schools had doubled as centers of social and civic activity are hanging somewhere between disadvantage and devastation.

So for eight years my mother tried to redirect some

of the state's money to restoring local elementary schools and equipping them with Internet and satellite technology to bring in resources from across the country. From the county school board she became active in the state school boards' association. She spent weeks in West Virginia's capitol and at meetings of the state board of education, arguing for a reformed policy. She eventually went to law school, in part to continue the same work. She wrote her first law-review article on the economies of scale standard. The first brief she wrote for West Virginia's supreme court contributed to a bold but unsuccessful suit to slow school consolidation.

Devotion's Unease

The source of my mother's work is, I think, the principle that understanding our dependences is a key to understanding our obligations. This means considering not only what we rely on for our own convenience, but what is required for the continued well-being of the achievements, practices, and values that we love most. Her efforts seem to me a reminder that working for what we love most is the furthest thing from self-indulgence or narcissism. It is sometimes a hard discipline, a reminder that the honest love of any good thing discomforts us so far as we find that thing neglected or despoiled around us. Her love of education has been a devotion to discomfort.

She loves education because she came on it hard. During more than a decade in the public and private

schools of Wilmington, Delaware, she now says that
she learned nothing more than how to take tests successfully. Later, as an undergraduate and graduate
student, she still found learning divorced from living.
The questions of scholarship fascinated her sometimes, but they did not help her to understand her
own life. They seemed neither to arise from nor to
return to the pleasures, fears, and projects that ani-
mate ordinary existence. They brought no maturity,
nothing that she could call (except that she avoids
any word that hints at sanctimony) wisdom. She left
the academy with only her uncompleted disserta-
tion between her and a professorship that she never
sought.

That departure ratified her gravest suspicions
about the gulf between learning and life. It also
marked a new effort to bring them together. That
hope drew her and my father to let my sister and me
guide our own learning as an element of our uncom-
monly free lives. We would learn out of life, they
hoped, and for life. Yet even as they carried out this
experiment, accepting the task of overseeing us every
hour of every day, my mother entered the politics of
public education with fresh energy. While she worked
to save and to improve public schools, she endeavored
as well to help her children learn in a better way than
she believed the schools could provide. To critics, she
was inconsistent. In fact, she was guided by a deeper
consistency: a commitment to supporting learning
wherever she could. Her love for education did not
begin or end in her love for her children; her love for

us inflected her work as a homeschooler, while her political work gave a different tone to the same, uniting motivation.

Thinking back, I believe that this period of my mother's life highlights an essential point: the aim that my father described as "making a corner of the world as sane as possible" means taking responsibility for what our loves rely upon. That responsibility took several forms for my parents: carrying out their commitments with rare integrity in their private lives, but also pursuing the same commitments in the community that they had made their own by settling in it. It might have been possible to achieve the first without looking beyond their own lives. The second is an acknowledgment that, in the end, there is nothing good that we can have alone.

There is much talk nowadays about the existence or nonexistence of "historical guilt." Generally, the phrase is used by those who oppose some policy, often affirmative action, that is alleged to rest on an idea of such guilt. Whatever one's judgment of all this, the fact remains that dedication to some hope or ideal means mourning its failures and working to prevent their repetition, even if they are inevitable in an imperfect world. Wendell Berry has written of his return to a landscape wrecked by his ancestors' poor farming, "A destructive history, once it is recognized as such, is a nearly insupportable burden. Understanding it is a disease of understanding, depleting the sense of efficacy and paralyzing effort, unless it finds healing work." He undertook his writing and restorative farming, Berry concludes, "to affirm my life as a thing decent in possibility."

We mourn the destruction or neglect of what we love, or understand to be good. When we comprehend our implication in destruction, love can create a burden almost beyond our strength. Yet the love that brings us the burden is also our only honest way, if not of shedding it, then of turning it to work that can present a counterpoint to destruction. Work should affirm our lives as things decent in possibility, against the keen perception of their possibilities of indecency. This alchemy of love into responsibility belongs at the heart of a renewed commitment to the commons.

Responsibility and Dignity

Through her years of political work, I never heard my mother describe herself as an activist. She was a mother and wife (just as my father would have described himself first as a father and husband), a gardener, a stenographer and then a lawyer, and a citizen who cared intensely about education. Far from being naive about her commitments, she can express cynical pessimism about the near-term prospects of her work and the character and motives of many of the people that she encounters in politics. She has never imagined, though, that cynicism or other people's disappointing behavior would excuse her from public responsibility. I do not mean that there is indignity in identifying oneself as an activist; but there is dignity in not needing that label to believe elementally that one's life includes public responsibility. That is one answer to the question of where politics has gone today.

The word *dignity* is not much used nowadays. It has its origins in the Latin *dignitas*, which referred to the title or position of a noble in a medieval aristocracy. *Dignitas* was not a quality or an achievement, but a status. Its possession commanded respect. A part of the aspiration of democracy is to grant everyone a part of dignity, to make citizenship mean membership in an aristocracy of equals. The idea of *human* dignity, so much a part of our modern commitments to ideas such as human rights, takes that idea a step further by asserting that just being a person should command respect.

Even in these uses there remains a hint of a very important idea: that dignity is not a universal fact, but a universal possibility. The condition of dignity, which does not just discourage others from dispossessing or torturing us—the narrowest aim of human rights—but elicits a positive respect, is an achievement. As defenders of human rights accurately perceive, we can be denied dignity by torturers, by censors, by secret police: this is the humiliation that the dissidents of Central Europe acted to resist. However, we can also deny dignity to ourselves. We can fail to achieve it.

The undignified character of much that we do is a part of the ironist's concern. Derivative phrases and feelings are worrisome because they make us seem fatuous and hollow, most of all to ourselves. *Wired*'s self-aggrandizing and *Fast Company*'s quest for authenticity are also motivated by dignity. They are

desperate answers to the increasingly pointed question of what kind of lives could enable us to take ourselves seriously. The elements of fantasy in their
answers have not, it must be said, dignified them.

Anyone, and especially a young person, must be
wary in taking up an intensely personal moral idea
such as dignity. The public advocates of virtue can
never escape a perception that, to a degree beyond
reasonableness and good taste, they are advertising
their own virtuous persons. Moreover, the more an
idea is bound up with a person's life and character, as
dignity is, the greater is the suspicion that insight into
it can come only with a long life. I am sure that both
of these dangers are real. What I want to offer,
though, is a tentative report, not at all of my own life,
but of what I have admired in people who have tried
to live well and, through decades of success and failure, have held on to a developing idea of what that
aim involves. Because I think that I have seen dignity
in their lives, I can attempt to say what it is I have
seen.

The dignity that I have observed has to do with the
harmony of commitment, knowledge, and work.
Commitment involves a clear sense of what a person
is devoted to, how one believes a life should be lived.
The simplest way to indignity is the acquiescent confusion that draws the current creed from the day's
broadcast signals. A person with this uncritical recep-
tivity can hardly even be present to another; when we
cannot sense another's orienting commitments, we
begin to suspect that we are not talking to anyone at

all. In contrast, a lifelong politician's devotion to "the harmed people," Adam Michnik's determination to put his life in the service of creating a Polish civil society, or Wendell Berry's decision to undertake the work of "a life decent in possibility," all reveal the power of knowing one's own purposes. In this respect, dignity depends on moral clarity.

This, though, is not enough. Moral clarity without knowledge of concrete things is the condition of fanatics such as Poland's Antoni Macerewicz, or more often of the well-intentioned and inept. It is not always clear which of these is more dangerous. What dignity I have seen eminently involves Isaiah Berlin's notion of "the sense of reality," an accurate perception of where one is set, and what currents of possibility and prohibition run there. It is a great achievement to be able to say of a proposal not "That sounds good," but "That's true" or "That won't work." Those are the phrases of a person who knows her field, literal or figurative, in a fashion that is almost sensory. She perceives the grain of possibility, the line and heft of danger, the obdurate certainty of what cannot be done. She has a special sense of what goes on around her. She knows what an event signifies, whether it announces a new opportunity or forecloses some hoped-for enterprise. She understands what an act is likely to accomplish, for good or bad. She often intuits why people behave as they do, without floundering in confused theories about their motives. As far as is possible, she clearly senses her own motives, powers, and limits.

Lacking this knowledge—really a kind of competence for living—invites mistaking our own hang-ups for the grounds of reality. It means imagining the world as a theater whose players are one's own desires and fears, pleasures, and revulsions. This is the basis, not least, of the indignity of moralizing. The moralizer sees others' failings, of whatever species especially fascinates him, at a degree of magnification that obscures their ambivalence and confusion in distended badness. He is obtuse to paradox, especially the paradox of his own implication, by sheer fascination or in more complex ways, with the perceived evils that he sets out to rebuke. He is the figure that Czeslaw Milosz labored to overcome by scrupulously documenting him in *The Captive Mind*. It is not necessary to speak here of angels, or of Bruce Babbitt at the Hobet 21 strip mine.

Acquiring the sense of reality often means tempering one's claims to moral clarity, or rather understanding that accurate perception can confound distinctions that might once have seemed obvious and thwart the impulse to self-righteousness. The sense of reality also moderates one's practical aspirations, the changes one seeks to foist upon the world. What it leaves, though, is tempered, cleansed of some impurities and hardened to the durability that a life's work requires. It is the ground for maintaining "the passionate pursuit of the real" that brought Milosz to, and beyond, his encounter with a generation of moralizers.

The idea of work, of activity, is the most important

of all. It is here that commitment and knowledge find expression or fall back into mere good intention. A person's work gives her purposes a body: a shape, a history of projects and products that carry them from the mind into the world. We know that this is where we are tested, where the seriousness of our purposes and the adequacy of our knowledge are up for general estimation. There is no mistaking the gap between professed principle and action in a person whose advertised commitments are betrayed by the shape of his life. Equally significant, though, is the substance that activity takes on when it represents both purpose and understanding. A marriage of commitment and knowledge produces dignified work.

I think of this achievement through the idea of the craftsman, perhaps because I have known craftsmen well and admired their work, perhaps because the solidity of their labor ties ideas to sound and reliable things. His enduring quality of dignity arises from the fact that his work is luminous to him, in its process and its purpose. He understands the application of every tool he uses; many of them he may be able to make or repair himself. He can judge the quality of his materials because he understands what they must contribute to his product and just how that contribution will be made. Because he understands the use of his product as well, he knows just what it is to make it well or badly.

What I have seen of dignity has been the partial achievement of an answer to the question: What is a worthy life for a person to lead? Trying to answer that question is a matter of both words and life, the expression of commitments and the performance of competent and good acts. The burden of this book is that both the purposes and the knowledge that guide our work should lead us, sometimes, to work for public things. So far as these are the sources of what we love, and form the conditions of our love's continuance, dignity requires an acknowledgment of the commons. This acknowledgment means understanding what we love well enough to understand also that our love implicates us in the well-being or degradation of the thousand things that preserve what we love. It is a practical devotion. It carries us forward into action that, even if it is not always pellucid, has some weight and some luminescence of its own.

The Sufficiency of Things

A dignified life, then, can offer a living defense of responsibility, earnestness, and honesty about the difficult relations between private lives and public well-being. One advantage of an ironic culture is that it does not permit earnest declaration to come cheap: to speak of high aims and not be merely high-minded requires having become the sort of person in whom those aims have some hope of reaching fruition. Skepticism about public life finds an answer not in mere declaration, but in people who make public responsibility an integral part of themselves. To establish the necessity of public things is only half the argument against the social withdrawal of the lifestyle enclave and the psychic withdrawal of unremitting irony; one must also establish that taking responsibility is viable. The full response to despair is not just to invoke hope, but to generate it.

People who undertake this sort of living maintain what I have called the moral ecology. By demonstrating that certain ways of living are possible, they invite others to live in the same ways. Living proof of possibility exercises a claim on the imagination that can become a claim on action. It calls us out of ourselves. We learn to shape our lives by answering these models, because in them we see what we might be, and find it good. In the absence of these examples, the possibility of such lives would slip away from us. Everything good in us has lived before, and nearly all is a direct gift from people who, often quietly, taught it to us as one might teach a craft, a dance, or the knowledge of a place: by permitting us to participate in it with them.

These lives are the source of the discipline that gives form to our affection, energy, and thought. It is a learned discipline, developed through acquaintance with people whose lives display its purposes. These people present us with moral arguments articulated in flesh and effort. Often, only knowing them can make it possible to speak confidently of the ideals that they enact. If we do not encounter such lives, the ideals may become unspeakable as well. To Czeslaw Milosz's unsettling observation that things unpronounced tend to nonexistence, it is necessary to add

that things nonexistent tend to silence or to babble—
to irony or to angels.

Above all, these people assure us that the real
world is not something to be fled, that it is sometimes
both sufficient and good. A great part of the appeal of
Wired and *Fast Company* is their contempt for banality, their insistence that their formula alone can give
life verve and thrill. In the same spirit, if in a very different tone, tales of angels and "re-enchantment" suggest that the world as we know it is insufficient,
desiccated, and weary. They both share this impa-
tience toward the world with the practitioners of flattening irony; but where the Free Agent and the angel
gazer rebel against the world's insufficiency, the ironist acquiesces to it. The rebels put their faith in the
belief that fantasy is both necessary and potent, that
only it can make life worth our attention. The self-
styled realists judge instead that nothing can qualify
life for serious attention.

Against this, good lives argue for the adequacy of
reality. They argue that our existence, with its limits,
entanglements, necessary dependences, and disappointments, is not to be escaped but to be contemplated more carefully and respectfully than it has been
our recent practice to do. That contemplation may
suggest that the mundane life—the life of the world—
has more that is good, and good partly because it is
necessary, than any fantasy can offer. It invites a
realignment of our moral imagination to what is near
at hand.

One way to this lies through an ambiguity in *irony*,

the word that has haunted this book. In its textbook sense, irony refers to the presence in a statement or experience of an unexpected meaning, a significance beyond and contrary to the obvious. Our contemporary irony shrugs off, doubts, and reassembles significance to drain words of evocation, beauty, and moral weight. It discovers behind the appearance of meaning the fact of insignificance. It is a static irony, a way of staying unmoved by our neighbors, the world, ourselves.

However, there is another kind of irony, which discovers a different sort of unexpected significance. It uncovers, in what is ordinarily imagined to be unimportant or banal, something that elicits surprise, delight, and reverence. What it uncovers is richer than what the rebellion against reality produces; above all, it is real. This irony is ecstatic, in the etymologically strict sense of drawing us out of our stasis. It is the irony of discovery. It moves us.

My father tells me that, in the evening, he watches my mother working in our garden, bent over her tomatoes. Now and again, she cocks an eye or gestures dramatically with a crooked finger. "Then," he says, "I know she has just made a point." She does her clearest thinking there, parsing arguments, working through problems as she pulls weeds, shakes the dirt from their roots, and throws them to the compost heap. I sometimes think that, for years after she left her graduate program in philosophy and came to West Virginia with my father, she must have resisted that union of thought and dirt. Thought resents the gnarled roots that trip it, the mud that sullies it, the endless tasks that stake it to a place and a routine. Thought wants the privilege of cleanliness, and the liberty to leave. Yet she has succeeded in embedding her thought thoroughly in the dirt, the growing things, and the labor of that place. Her thought, which might once have carried her away, is now her way to stay. The shape of her thought is her concern for her place, her love for it, and her fear for its future, and so her devotion to the work that its maintenance requires.

She is not alone. I know people in West Virginia who devote in each year a month, or two or three, to environmental and other politics. Some of them have become the state's most knowledgeable experts on the law and ecology of mining, of toxic chemicals, of land-filling. They are the ones who have resisted strip-mining year after year. They are familiar sights in the halls of the state legislature, and in the meeting rooms of the Division of Environmental Protection. Yet when I think of them, I see them in their places, between walls that some of them have built, among trees and bushes, ferns and herbs and wildflowers. It is their delight in these living places that carries them to their work. Theirs are lives lived well enough, and thoughtfully enough, to sustain public work whose reward is more the knowledge of responsibility fulfilled than the satisfaction of victory won. Their care for the places they know best moves them to act beyond those places, to preserve the possibility of care in their own and other lives.

Although I am younger than they are, I have felt some of the same experience. I cannot understand destruction without conceiving of the destruction of the farm where I grew up and still spend as much time as I am able, without imagining its slopes stripped and collapsed. I cannot think of the importance of preservation without seeing the health that is still in those worn hills, and considering what would be required to maintain it. The physical work that is there, digging, splitting firewood, and scything brush, seems to me the most necessary, somehow even the most real, that I have known. I can work at it for days, and be restored. It moves me.

West Virginia, in most minds, is far from what I am describing. It is a place marked by what it lacks: culture, education, wealth. It is a place of poverty, deprivation, a place *without*. This is the expected West Virginia. The one that I am describing is unexpected, but it is real. Its reality emerges in the knowing. This is the knowledge that comes with working oneself into a place or a vocation, a labor or a love. It is a dedication of oneself.

In dedicating ourselves, in accepting responsibility, we cultivate a special quality of perception. This is the habit of seeing things in their complex mutual dependence, and understanding how what we most value is implicated in that web. The corollary of recognizing dependence in this way is a sense of gratitude and wonder that so much has gone into the upkeep of what sustains and delights us. In this condition, sometimes, understanding and wonder can grow together.

This is at the same time a way to the sobering recognition of our capacity for destruction, and of the potency of neglect. It is a reminder of the destructive legacy that can become unbearable, and of the importance of limiting our part in destruction. Perceiving this can carry us across the gap between indifference and intelligent devotion. It is possible to know things in a way that carries us into them, that draws us to adapt ourselves to their forms and requirements. This might be called a reverent knowledge, in which knowledge deepens the intelligence of love, and makes it more adequate to reality.

Seeing things as they weave into one another reveals the structure of dependences that makes devotion intelligible. We can undo that vision by stripping, flattening irony or by the impulse to leave behind all that we have been before and declare our private sufficiency. In the end, the two amount to the same privation, for they are similarly deprived of sustenance. When we refuse both those choices, we work instead to preserve some of the wholeness of things, including the things we have in common, because we have been moved by them. Because we attend to their wholeness, they sometimes move us again.

Emerson distinguished in public and intellectual life between "the party of memory and the party of hope." That distinction does not fit us well today. The parties of foolish optimism and idle pessimism alike share forgetfulness and neglect of our dependences and the responsibilities that accompany them. Hope in such a time comes partly from recollection, gathering to ourselves the things that we have lost or are in danger of losing. Betterment remains the great possibility of public life. Preservation, including the preservation of public life itself, is its great necessity. The party of hope cannot continue today unless it is also the party of memory.

We need today a kind of thought and action that is too little contemplated yet remains possible. It is the kind aimed at the preservation of what we love most in the world, and a stay against forgetting what that love requires. It is an exercise of margins against boundlessness, of earned hope against casual despair, and of responsibility against heedlessness. If it appears conservative, that is because we have begun to forget the conditions necessary to betterment. If it appears radical, that is because we have neglected the conditions necessary to conservation. The common origin of its personal practice and public project is the maintenance of a world, natural and social, that moves us to participate in and protect it, and of the human character that can be so moved. It is a slow, unceasing work whose ground and aim is ecstasy.

Acknowledgments

THIS BOOK would not have been written without the encouragement and support of Bob Kuttner and Paul Starr at the *American Prospect*, the ever-insightful guidance of Pratap Mehta at Harvard, or the friendship and provocation of Brady Case, David Grewal, and Sidney Kwiram. I am also indebted to Steve Grand of the German Marshall Fund for making possible my time in Central Europe, and to Ash Green, Leyla Aker, and Marco Simons for judicious editing.

Selected Bibliography

Preface

Mann, Thomas, as quoted in *W. B. Yeats: Selected Poetry*. Ed. Timothy Webb. London: Penguin, 1991.

Chapter One: Avoiding the World

Allison, Dorothy. *Bastard Out of Carolina*. New York: Plume, 1992.

Carter, Bill. "Seinfeld Says It's All Over, and It's No Joke for NBC." *New York Times,* 26 December 1997, sec. A, p. 1.

Coupland, Douglas. *Generation X*. New York: St. Martin's Press, 1991.

———. *Life After God*. New York: Pocket Books, 1994.

Emerson, Ralph Waldo. "Self-Reliance," in *Ralph Waldo Emerson*. Ed. Richard Poirier. New York: Oxford University Press, 1990.

Freud, Sigmund. *Introductory Lectures on Psycho-analysis*. Trans. James Strachey. New York: Norton, 1996.

Goldman, Karen. *Angel Voices: The Advanced Handbook for Aspiring Angels*. New York: Simon and Schuster, 1997.

Kelly, Kevin. "What Would McLuhan Say?" *Wired,* issue 4.10 (October 1996).

Marx, Karl. *The Eighteenth Brumaire of Louis Bonaparte*. New York: International Publishers, 1994.

McCourt, Frank. *Angela's Ashes: A Memoir*. New York: Scribner's, 1996.

Moore, Thomas. *Care of the Soul: A Guide for Cultivating Depth and Sacredness in Everyday Life*. New York: HarperCollins, 1994.

———. *The Re-Enchantment of Everyday Life*. New York: HarperCollins, 1997.

Muoio, Anna. "Boss Management." In Fast Company [online]. Available at http://www.fastcompany.com/online/resources/unitofone.html.

Peters, Tom. "Brand You." In Fast Company [online]. Available at http://www.fastcompany.com/brandyou/story.html.

Pink, Daniel H. "Free Agent Nation." *Fast Company,* issue 12 (December 1997): 131.

Regis, Ed. "Meet the Extropians." *Wired,* issue 2.10 (October 1994).

Schueman, Helen. *A Course in Miracles*. New York: Viking, 1996.

Somaygi, Stephen. "He's the Voice of the Tiananmen Generation." *Fast Company,* issue 10 (August 1997): 32.

Sterling, Bruce. "Greetings from Burning Man!" *Wired,* issue 4.11 (November 1996).

Taylor, William, and Alan Webber. "What's Fast?" *Fast Company,* issue 20 (December 1998): 16.

Terry, Sara. "John Norquist." *Fast Company,* issue 20 (December 1998): 158.

Thoreau, Henry David. *Walden*. New York: Random House, 1983.

Weber, Max. "Science as a Vocation." *From Max Weber*. New York: Oxford University Press, 1946.

Wilde, Oscar, as quoted in Lionel Trilling, *Sincerity and Authenticity*. Cambridge: Harvard University Press, 1973.

Wired (introductory quote), issue 2.10 (October 1994).

Chapter Two: The Absence of Politics

Baker, Peter. "Clinton Calls for Dialogue on Race." *Washington Post,* 15 June 1997, sec. A, p. 1.

———. "President Mulls National Apology for Slavery." *Washington Post,* 16 June 1997, sec. A, p. 1.

———. "Clinton Calls a Summit on Internet Smut: Voluntary Plan Urged to Protect Children." *Washington Post,* 12 July 1997, sec. A, p. 6.

Clinton, Hillary. Lecture delivered at the University of Texas, Austin, 6 April 1993.

Glazer, Nathan. "In Defense of Preference." *The New Republic,* (6 April 1998): 18–20.

Harris, John F. "A Presidential Push for Helping Hands: Past, Present Leaders Open Volunteer Summit." *Washington Post,* 28 April 1997, sec. A, p. 1.

Marx, Karl. *The German Ideology.* New York: International Publishers, 1978.

Montaigne, Michel de. *The Essays.* Trans. Donald Frame. Stanford: Stanford University Press, 1995.

Orwell, George. "Why I Write," in *The Orwell Reader.* New York: Harcourt Brace, 1984.

Rousseau, Jean-Jacques. *On the Social Contract.* Trans. Judith R. Masters. New York: St. Martin's Press, 1978.

Chapter Three: The Practice of the Public

Berry, Wendell. "A Native Hill," in *Recollected Essays, 1965–1980.* San Francisco: North Point Press, 1981.

Hardin, Garrett. "The Tragedy of the Commons." *Science,* issue 168 (1968): 143–48.

Havel, Vaclav. "Politics and Conscience," in *Open Letters:*

Selected Papers, ed. and trans. Paul Wilson. London: Faber and Faber, 1991.

———. "The Power of the Powerless," ibid.

Macerewicz, Antoni. Personal interview, Warsaw, Poland, June 1998.

Michnik, Adam. *Gazeta Wyborcza,* 23 March 1993.

Milton, John. *Paradise Lost.* New York: Norton, 1975.

Murray, Charles. *What It Means to Be a Libertarian: A Personal Interpretation.* New York: Broadway Books, 1997.

Chapter Four: The Law of the Land: Political Choice and Attentiveness

Babbitt, Bruce. Address delivered at the Hobet 21 coal mine in West Virginia, 3 August 1996.

McGinley, Patrick. Personal interview, West Virginia University, May 1998.

Milosz, Czeslaw. *The Captive Mind.* Trans. Jane Zielonko. London: Penguin, 1981.

Personal interview with anonymous OSM officer, May 1998.

Chapter Five: The Neighbor and the Machine: Technology and Responsibility

Frost, Robert. *The Poetry of Robert Frost.* Ed. Edward C. Lathem. New York: Henry Holt & Co., 1987.

Kelly, Kevin. *Out of Control: The Rise of Neo-Biological Civilization.* New York: Addison-Wesley, 1994.

Kitcher, Philip. *The Lives to Come: The Genetic Revolution and Human Possibilities,* 209–15. New York: Simon & Schuster, 1996.

Levinson, Paul. "The Extinction of Extinction." *Wired,* issue 1.04 (September–October 1993).

Silver, Lee M. *Remaking Eden: Cloning and Beyond in a Brave New World.* New York: Avon Books, 1997.

Simpson, Roderick. "Cloning. Problem? No Problem." *Wired,* issue 5.09 (September 1997).

Thoreau, Henry David. *Walden.* New York: Random House, 1983.

Index

A NOTE ABOUT THE AUTHOR

Jedediah Purdy was born and home-educated on a hillside farm in rural West Virginia. He entered high school at fourteen and after graduating spent a year in environmental politics in his home state, dividing his time between public policy and community work. Purdy attended college at Harvard, where he studied the history of ideas and moral and political philosophy. Since finishing his degree, he has concentrated on writing essays on culture and politics, and is currently studying law, environment, and values at Yale.

A NOTE ON THE TYPE

The text of this book was set in Sabon, a typeface designed by Jan Tschichold (1902–1974), the well-known German typographer. Based loosely on the original designs by Claude Garamond (c. 1480–1561), Sabon is unique in that it was explicitly designed for hotmetal composition on both the Monotype and Linotype machines as well as for filmsetting. Designed in 1966 in Frankfurt, Sabon was named for the famous Lyons punch cutter Jacques Sabon, who is thought to have brought some of Garamond's matrices to Frankfurt.

Composed by Creative Graphics,
Allentown, Pennsylvania
Printed and bound by R. R. Donnelley and Sons,
Harrisonburg, Virginia
Designed by Virginia Tan